THE COMMUNITARIAN PERSUASION

THE
COMMUNITARIAN
PERSUASION

PHILIP SELZNICK

Foreword by Michael J. Lacey

WOODROW WILSON CENTER PRESS
WASHINGTON, D.C.

DISTRIBUTED BY THE JOHNS HOPKINS UNIVERSITY PRESS
BALTIMORE AND LONDON

EDITORIAL OFFICES

Woodrow Wilson Center Press
One Woodrow Wilson Plaza
1300 Pennsylvania Avenue, N.W.
Washington, D.C. 20004-3027
Telephone 202-691-4010
www.wilsoncenter.org

Distributed by:

The Johns Hopkins University Press
P.O. Box 50370
Baltimore, Maryland 21211
Telephone 1-800-537-5487
www.press.jhu.edu

2 4 6 8 9 7 5 3 1

Library of Congress Cataloging in Publication Data

Selznick, Philip, 1919–
    The communitarian persuasion / Philip Selznick ; foreword by Michael J. Lacey
    p. cm.
    Includes index.
    ISBN 1-930365-05-5 (cloth : alk. paper) — ISBN 1-930365-06-3 (pbk. : alk. paper)
    1. Communitarianism. 2. Communitarianism—United States. I. Title.
HM758 .S45 2002
307—dc21
2001007634

ABOUT THE CENTER

The Center is the living memorial of the United States of America to the nation's twenty-eighth president, Woodrow Wilson. Congress established the Woodrow Wilson Center in 1968 as an international institute for advanced study, "symbolizing and strengthening the fruitful relationship between the world of learning and the world of public affairs." The Center opened in 1970 under its own board of trustees.

In all its activities the Woodrow Wilson Center is a nonprofit, nonpartisan organization, supported financially by annual appropriations from the Congress, and by the contributions of foundations, corporations, and individuals. Conclusions or opinions expressed in Center publications and programs are those of the authors and speakers and do not necessarily reflect the views of the Center staff, fellows, trustees, advisory groups, or any individuals or organizations that provide financial support to the Center.

For Doris

CONTENTS

FOREWORD

We can all use some help in thinking more cogently about politics and government, and no matter how experienced the reader, this book will provide it. It is directed to a thoughtful, literate, busy public. It wastes no room or time. Yet despite its small size, it is a big book, and a good deal more than a primer. Written by one of America's most distinguished social theorists, it presents in skillful and unobtrusive fashion all the really fundamental ideas and principles required for satisfactory address to a large and many-faceted problem, for "facing up to modernity" as our author puts it.[1]

This is not to say that there is no work ahead for the reader, only that the work will be rewarded. Every thinking person understands what Einstein had in mind when he advised the science writer to "make it as simple as possible, but no simpler." Far too much of our talk about the public and its problems is cluttered with half-truths in the service of false choices, always in the name of lofty ideals. We

---

1. For a collection of scholarly essays exploring Philip Selznick's thought and its influence, see Robert A. Kagan, Martin Krygier, and Kenneth Winston, eds., *Legality and Community: On the Intellectual Legacy of Philip Selznick* (Berkeley, Calif.: Rowman and Littlefield; Berkeley Public Policy Press, 2002). My own essay in that collection, "Taking Ideals Seriously: Philip Selznick and the Natural Law Tradition," draws attention to the affinities between Selznick's approach to a sociologically informed moral philosophy and older traditions of natural law as the framework for politics and morals.

may feel the urge to resist—but how, exactly? Better criticism, of the sort we need for really constructive work, requires a higher viewpoint than we can normally muster. We know that splitting the difference between half–truths and untethered ideals is not the way to go. As Selznick points out, "we cannot protect ideals we do not understand," and to understand them properly we need to go back to the basics of our social and political experience. We need to see things whole and in their connections.

Out of this need there arises the search for a public philosophy up to the level of the times, and in what follows Selznick contributes something essential to the equipment required for that journey—part map, part monitor, a kind of positioning system for negotiating the complex social geography of today. A public philosophy is not a neat and tidy thing. It bears too much traffic for that. It is the inherited framework of ideas and values that provides the intellectual infrastructure for our politics. Like other kinds of infrastructure, we may well take it for granted and neglect to make the investments needed to keep it really serviceable. Too much of this, and our public affairs become congested and backed up. We get the sense that the political world itself is stalling out. A feeling of torpor and collective impotence settles over the public. So things seem to stand at the moment.

The American public philosophy is of course part and parcel of the broader liberal tradition of the West, whence it came. This inheritance, too, has its complexities, its ambiguities and contradictions, and yet it is the proximate source of our highest social and political ideals. As Selznick points out, "liberalism is a many-stranded tradition, not a well-defined ideology or a tight system of premises and conclusions." Its development has not been peaceful, orderly, or particularly clear from the standpoint of the history of ideas. From the beginning the sharpest conflicts in American politics have occurred not between liberals and those committed to genuinely different traditions, such as conservative paternalism in the Tory style, for example, or socialism or communism, but rather between people stressing different strands and fragments of the liberal tradition itself, as many scholarly observers have noted over the years.

Our conservatives are liberals of a kind. Strictly speaking, most of them tend to be classical liberals in the academic sense of the phrase, where *classical* refers to the continuing vitality of the arguments that began in the seventeenth century with John Milton, John

Locke, and other architects of the case for civil and religious liberty as against the claims and conventions of the old order, with its monarchy, hereditary rule, and fusion of church and state. As conservatives they are devoted to limited and minimal government, the more local the better. They are committed to individual liberty and private property. They are trustful for the most part that the natural dynamics of civil society are benign, less prone to corruption and injustice if left alone than would be the case in the aftermath of "government interference," as the point is normally put. When under pressure and in need of first principles, the conservative temptation of today is to reach out to far more modern libertarian, free market ideas, pure and simple.

These ideas are purer and simpler not necessarily in a technical sense, for even the most casual acquaintance with university-based neoclassical economic theory or rational choice theory in political science would belie that notion. Rather, they are purer and simpler in the sense that they are unencumbered by the kinds of social and moral constraints, implicit and explicit, that were taken for granted by their classical forerunners. The upshot is a rather rigid, one-dimensional perspective on the role of government in modern culture, from within which it is possible only grudgingly and without a clear conscience to endorse as truly legitimate most of the programs and policies of national government that have been put in place since the New Deal era and the Great Society that followed it. These doubts about the underlying legitimacy of today's "big government" are expressed in the ready resort to some combination of ideas about privatization and decentralization as the sovereign remedies for curing all the ills of governance in the new millennium.

If our conservatives are liberals of a sort, then what of our self-professed liberals? Our liberals tend to be, well . . . what *do* they tend to be? Worry about that gave birth to this book and provides the starting point for Selznick's inquiry. As conservatives have pounded home their case against government in recent decades, liberals have done what they could in response, typically by arguing that markets, too, are prone to misrule, and are so different in kind from government institutions that they cannot, in the nature of things, be a very good substitute. But when contemporary liberals reach back for first principles, where do they turn? Increasingly, so it appears to Selznick, they turn to rather poorly grounded assertions about the nature of modern rights and the character of the state that must administer them. In doing so, they neglect earlier ways of thinking about the proper role of government. In consequence, they are unclear about the links of rights and duties, and thus adrift in their thinking about policy and governance.

Selznick's work represents the encounter of an older way with the newer ones. He writes from within the tradition of American pragmatism and the social and moral theory inspired by it. He is the architect of some of its most important postwar achievements. While he has been there all along, the new interest that others are now taking in his thought is part of the ongoing rediscovery of pragmatism in American thinking more generally. From the vantage point of pragmatic social theory Selznick concludes that today's liberal ethos is troubled deep down, having lost its bearings and sense of duty with respect to the fundamental requirements of community life. Welfare liberalism in the forms it has been given since the 1970s stands in need of basic correction no less than the conservative ethos does. In this at least what the two philosophies share is more important than what divides them. They share a basic weakness that experience has taught thoughtful critics to see as the main, recurrent sore spot in the liberal tradition as a whole—the loss, and thus the lack in recent times, of a well-grounded theory and ethic of responsibility.

That is the core problem dealt with in this book. Selznick believes that the most responsible form of modern liberalism is what he calls "communitarian liberalism." It is distinct from neoconservatism in all its forms and also from what welfare liberalism has come to mean in the minds of many in recent decades. Selznick's quarrel with welfare liberalism is not about whether modern government should be big and active. He knows it must be. He has always insisted that limited government need not be minimal. One of his principal works, *Law and Society in Transition: Towards Responsive Law,* which appeared in 1978 at the height of the many-angled crisis of authority from which we have still not fully recovered, stands up well as a framework in jurisprudence for understanding sympathetically what was at stake in the new demands on government that were registered by the social movements of those confusing and divisive days.

Selznick's quarrel with welfare liberalism is about something subtler and more fundamental. It concerns the intellectual foundations of contemporary liberalism, which he believes have become insecure due the influence of new styles of thought without roots in pragmatism, which have taken hold in the academy in recent decades. Here the main targets are the rather different and very complex liberalisms of John Rawls and Ronald Dworkin. Their influence in political philosophy and jurisprudence has come with a heavy cost from the standpoint of the ideals involved in pragmatic moral theory and social analysis. Together they have buttressed the rationale for a "rights-centered liberalism" that fails to speak adequately to duties or to a view of the theoretical grounds for a just government that holds that no matter how big and active it may be, the state must be neutral with respect to moral conflicts in culture, and not involved in shaping the moral order. Though neither thinker intended it (indeed, they would vigorously deny the charge), the influence of their work upon the liberal ethos has contributed to the relativism and extremism with respect to the value of personal autonomy that have been under attack since the 1980s. These are intellectual vulnerabilities that handicap a politics in search of social justice and the common good.

This is what the debate between welfare liberals and communitarians is all about, and Selznick is decidedly on the side of the communitarians. He prefers the political philosophy of John Dewey to those of Rawls or Dworkin, and thus he seeks amendment of what welfare liberalism has become, not repudiation of the historical achievements that went into the rise of postwar government. The goal is to reestablish a sense of ordered liberty, a better balance between the needs of the person and those of the community, so that they might flourish together. Selznick chooses "communitarian liberalism" as a label for the outlook to make it clear that the ideals of the liberal tradition, as he understands them, do not stand opposed to the ideals of community. On the contrary, their fates are profoundly intertwined.

The Communitarian Persuasion is a reflection, nourished by decades of participation in the leadership of social science research, about the nature of our modern social fabric, about the cultural changes (generally favorable changes, by the way, despite their disruptions) that continue to stress and fray the fabric, and about what must be done to restore its resiliency. The raw material of our social fabric is the innate readiness for mutual obligation that grows naturally out of our dependence upon one another for the basic goods of life. This readiness takes specific shape in the routines of family, school, church, and working life. Gradually it becomes the sense or feeling of responsibility—the moral sense, if you like, through which we regulate our relations and fulfill our loyalties. It is not a constant or a simple feeling. The moral sense can be mistaken, misdirected, and abused. Sociologically speaking, the sense of responsibility changes in response to the ways people think about and evaluate it, for these ways add up to the subtle processes that alter the moral environment of culture. Selznick speaks of responsibility as "the psychic tissue of community," and his book is an extended meditation on its meaning and reach, an exploration of its different dimensions, personal, social, and institutional. Because Selznick thinks about responsibility in a more sustained and focused way than most of our writers on society and politics, *The Communitarian Persuasion* deserves a place on the bookshelf alongside the works of Croly, Lippmann, Dewey, Sandel, Taylor, and others who have shaped our understanding of public philosophy.

COMMUNITARIANS AND THE PROGRESSIVE TRADITION

The Irish have a saying that "a man's tradition is that part of him that is older than he is." This way of looking at it captures the point that any tradition is really alive only to the degree that it has been personally appropriated by the living. Are they capable of giving a forceful account of its rationale, forceful most importantly to themselves? If not, how can they, or anyone else, manage to live by it? We grow up and into our traditions. We struggle with them to ensure that they fit the needs of the present, revising what needs revision, augmenting what was there but perhaps insufficiently developed, still never abandoning what was and is essential to the integrity of the inheritance. Here, too, the sense of responsibility is in operation. Traditions deal with and circumscribe the big questions of life. We must not end up, as the poet Szymborska put it, offering "apologies to great questions for small answers," the most common and worrisome of human failings.

Selznick is not writing history in *The Communitarian Persuasion*. He is speaking to contemporaries about how to make sense of the present, laying out his own formulation of responsible replies to the big questions of community life that are entailed in our being modern together. He acknowledges that the communitarian movement with which he is associated makes no particular claims to originality, and indeed there is about the movement an air of recovery, of return to older and better ways, closer to the experience of ordinary people than welfare liberalism. It is worth noting that the kind of liberalism that grew up in America roughly between the time of the Civil War and World War II was not a hotchpotch of relativism and self-assertion, as conservative critics often claim. It had its warrants, as Dewey would have put it, good reasons for its claims, and these came out of disciplined thought in philosophy and social science.

There is a deeper history to communitarian liberalism, in other words. That history includes the intellectual resources of a body of thought about the nature of community and government that gave coherence and continuity to the public philosophy of the long Progressive Era that extended from the late nineteenth century through the New Deal. Selznick knows it well and nods in its direction in his opening chapter with his brief remarks on voices kindred to those of today's communitarians, a grouping which includes the "new liberals" of an earlier time. One of the intellectual commitments that was "new" in the new liberalism of yesterday was its own communitarian turn, and the reasoning upon which that turn was based. The new liberalism arose out of the critique of laissez-faire economics, social Darwinism, and the strong individualist biases in the natural rights doctrines of its time. New liberals in the progressive mode of social theorizing sought not to abandon the values of classical liberalism, but rather, as Selznick hopes to do in response to the excessive individualism of the present, to amend them in order to adapt them to the new environment.[2]

---

2. For a concise discussion of the sources, contents, and influence of the new liberalism in government and culture, see Mary O. Furner, "Policy Knowledge: The New Liberalism," in *International Encyclopedia of Social and Behavioral Sciences,* edited by Neil J. Smelser and Paul B. Baltes (Oxford: Elsevier Science, 2001). See also Michael J. Lacey and Mary O. Furner, eds., *The State and Social Investigation in Britain and the United States* (New York: Woodrow Wilson Center Press and Cambridge University Press, 1993). Note particularly the opening chapter on relations between the growth of knowledge and the rise of modern government, "Social Investigation, Social Knowledge and the State: An Introduction" (pp. 3–60), and Furner's chapter "The Republican Tradition and the New Liberalism: Social Investigation, State Building and Social Learning in the Gilded Age" (pp. 171–241). Another essay by Furner examines the new liberal viewpoint in action with respect to the key problem of the Progressive period, the rights of labor. See her "Knowing Capitalism: Public Investigation and the Labor Question in the Long Progressive Era," in *The State and Economic Knowledge: The American and British Experiences,* edited by Mary O. Furner and Barry Supple (New York: Woodrow Wilson Center

The new liberalism was carried in large part by the leadership of the early social science disciplines, which were just emerging from the moral philosophy of the antebellum period and taking on separate identities as fields of research and writing. The liberal tradition was modernizing from within, in response to powerful social movements aimed at addressing the gathering social and economic miseries spawned by the industrial revolution. These problems were brought into focus via new forms of social empiricism, devised by both government bureaus and private agencies, which measured, monitored, and reported upon them. Working often in league with women and labor reformers, new liberals sought new kinds of protection for families and working-class communities. The most important lines of inquiry and argument to come out of these early encounters with the costs of modernity are those known to historians as pragmatism and instrumentalism in philosophy, institutionalism in economics, and the quest for a "sociological jurisprudence," which involved both sociology and law.

The gallery of new liberal ancestors would be large and in its own way diverse. To mention only the most important contributors to the legacy, it would include these names:

Henry Carter Adams, Lester F. Ward, John Wesley Powell, Carroll D. Wright, Richard Ely, Charles Horton Cooley, E. A. Ross, Josiah Royce, William James, George Herbert Mead, Jane Addams, Mary Parker Follett, E. R. A. Seligman, John R. Commons, Charles Beard, Charles Merriam, Roscoe Pound, Rev. John A. Ryan, W. E. B. DuBois, Herbert Croly, Walter Lippmann, and John Dewey.

Press and Cambridge University Press, 1990), pp. 241–286. While there is no comprehensive history of the new liberalism as an international phenomenon, Daniel T. Rogers outlines its contours in the social politics of the transatlantic reform communities that were in communication with one another in the Progressive Era in his *Atlantic Crossings: Social Politics in a Progressive Age* (Cambridge, Mass.: Harvard University Press, 1998). James T. Kloppenberg probes the work of many key theorists in his *Uncertain Victory: Social Democracy and Progressivism in European and American Thought, 1870–1920* (New York: Oxford University Press, 1986). Eldon J. Eisenach's *Lost Promise of Progressivism* (Lawrence: University Press of Kansas, 1994) is an exploration of the continuing relevance of the thinking of the Progressive Era to current debates over individual rights and civic responsibilities, the relationship between government and the economy, and the religious currents at work in the Progressive mentality.

Despite the differences among these people, all were committed to the pursuit of social justice through social science and philosophy. None was a moral relativist. All converged on the need to "think institutionally" if we are to think fruitfully about resolving social problems. All were convinced that the basic challenge facing modern government would be the need to deal with competition, sorting out its desirable forms from those which would undermine the common good, finding ways to secure its social benefits without succumbing to its built-in tendencies to oligarchy, domination, and weakening the bonds of community.[3]

The new liberals were sifting through the mixed blessings of modernity, and they looked, not exclusively but without any hesitation, to government to secure the results. In the dynamic, unpredictable, intensely competitive world of modern capitalism, government would be the only hope for regulating "the moral plane of competition," as Henry Carter Adams put it at the beginning of the new liberal tradition.[4] Living up to this responsibility would call for devising new bodies of knowledge, new competencies within government, new theories of law and regulation that could help to monitor and mediate the tradeoffs involved in the pursuit of economic efficiency and social justice. Understanding and control of the modern corporation was a top agenda item, as was the understanding and control of public authority through bureaucracy.

The ideal sought was not so much big government, in the sense given the term by the New Deal and the Great Society, although all new liberals would insist that it be no smaller than necessary to get its jobs done. Rather, the ideal was knowledgeable government, focused on the actual conditions and needs of the community. Connected to conversations about what the moral standards of an industrial community should be, the new liberal state was an organic part

3. For a discussion of the centrality of the willingness to "think institutionally" in defining the patterns of opposition in the history of American public philosophy, see Michael J. Lacey, "Federalism and National Planning: The Nineteenth Century Legacy," in *The American Planning Tradition: Culture and Policy*, edited by Robert Fishman (Baltimore: Woodrow Wilson Center Press and Johns Hopkins University Press, 2000), pp. 89–145.

4. For the classic introductory statement from the mid-1880s of the new liberal ethos and its outlook on government, competition, and social morality, see Joseph Dorfman, ed., *Relation of the State to Industrial Action and Economics and Jurisprudence: Two Essays by Henry Carter Adams* (New York: Columbia University Press, 1954).

of the community. It was not working from the outside in to impose burdensome rules on the people. As Dewey came to see the matter, the state was cooperating in long-range processes of social learning through politics, assisting in the development and expression of collective intelligence and responsibility. In doing so, to use Dewey's idiom, government helped to transform the "great society" of modernity, the volatile world of big enterprise, powerful organizations, and incessant innovation, into "the great community" of a healthy democratic social order.[5]

This is the tradition of inquiry and effort that Philip Selznick grew up and into, and to which he has contributed more than his share. He long ago mastered the philosophical currents involved, and together with his earlier book *The Moral Commonwealth* (1992), *The Communitarian Persuasion* takes communitarian liberalism further than Dewey took it, bringing its ethical and institutional aspects into sharper focus. Selznick's more technical scholarly works in the sociology of law, particularly his work with Philippe Nonet, *Law and Society in Transition: Towards Responsive Law* (1978), represent the most important analytical contributions to the search for a "sociological jurisprudence" since Roscoe Pound announced the need for it at the height of the Progressive Era.[6] His classic study *Leadership in Administration: A Sociological Interpretation* (1957) takes pragmatic social and moral theory into the world of bureaucracy, public and private. It developed the notions of organizational

---

5. Dewey's treatment of this transformation appears in his own most important contribution to public philosophy, *The Public and Its Problems* (New York: Henry Holt, 1927).

6. As a theme in the history of jurisprudence, sociological jurisprudence is about the sources of law in social experience. It looks to the empirical context of experience, but also to the ideals implicit in that context. It results in the view that there is a didactic and self-correcting quality to law in society, that law arises from experience developed by reason and in turn invites reasonable criticisms as its dictates are experienced in the life of society. Thus, law is an agency not simply of social control, but of social learning as well. For the history of the search for a sociological jurisprudence and its relations to other schools of jurisprudence in the first half of the twentieth century, see the running commentaries provided in Roscoe Pound, *Jurisprudence*, 5 vols. (St. Paul: West Publishing, 1959). For Selznick's contribution to this tradition, his formulation of "responsive law," and its context in recent scholarship in the fields of comparative law and legal development, see Robert A. Kagan's introduction to the new edition of Selznick and Nonet's *Law and Society in Transition: Towards Responsive Law* (New Brunswick, N.J.: Transaction Publishers, 2001), pp. vii–xxvi.

character and integrity as the most important concerns of institutional life, and laid out the argument that the interpretation and embodiment of values was the really essential dimension of genuine leadership, something related to but also different from managerial competence, something higher and more exacting.

Unlike those conservatives who harbor misgivings about the legitimacy of the whole corpus of programs and policies built up in the federal government over the past half-century, Selznick is inclined to accept them as the legitimate outcome of the search for a more satisfactory democratic order—a search that, in the nature of things, is never over. He is far from complacent about them, however, and offers us some new ways of thinking about what they actually do and how they might be improved. He makes it clear why we should be aiming not at deregulation, but at better regulation of a less suspicious and distrustful sort, and what the social principles underlying better regulation are. He is not opposed in principle to any responsible form of decentralization, nor is he deceived about its prospects as a cure-all. He has important new things to say about federalism as a principle of complex community life as well as a principle of government organization, and thus points to the need to get beyond either/or thinking with respect to relations between the nation and the states.

When you add up the operations of all the American governments, the federal institutions and those of the states and lesser civil divisions, the total is very large indeed. What are they doing? What kind of complex community are they trying to achieve? Selznick is not scandalized by the notion that big government and big competence are necessary to the attainment of big virtue, as are big resources. Nor is he hostile to the idea of the market, which has a great many things to commend it. But as his critique makes clear, intelligence and responsibility are not among them. He shows that it is not the market, but the market mentality that we have to fear if we want to face up to modernity. *The Communitarian Persuasion* explains how that neoliberal mentality often works and what we must be on guard against.

Like many conservatives, Selznick sings the praises of civil society, but he reminds us that its institutions, too, need civilizing through law and regulation. Throughout his book Selznick returns repeatedly to the idea that the aim of our public policies should be to shore up the fraying bonds of community. The virtues and blessings of social life that once could be left to the habits of tradition may now require help in the form of better institutional design if they are to flourish. We should not be deterred from the challenges of institutional design by artificial boundaries. His adversaries are theorists who erect artificial boundaries and impede the search for the common good. For communitarian liberalism, Selznick insists, the integration of law, government, and society is the desirable and practical ideal, not their separation. It seeks collaboration among them. The aim is stewardship of institutions capable of being responsive without capitulating in the rough world of political conflict, capable of what Selznick calls shared and self-correcting governance.

COMMUNITARIAN LIBERALISM AND RELIGION

This is complex and difficult work, and the workers require all the help they can get. One of the frayed bonds of community that Selznick seeks particularly to mend is the one that connects communitarian liberalism to the life and experience of religious communities. Here, too, he goes beyond Dewey and would push back the limits of Dewey's naturalism. In his last chapter Selznick reflects on the close connections between communitarian ideas and the teachings of religious communities. He invites us to think through with him what attitudes and beliefs, what articles of faith, what lessons of history come into play when we consider that question. His reflections mark something new at work in the spirit of the times. Modern liberalism has always made much of the need for civility, Selznick points out, but it has had a hard time appreciating the benefits of piety, particularly the carefully cultivated kind that makes up the practice of spirituality in the great religious traditions.

Though Dewey himself rejected militant atheism, he was comfortably at home with the nonmilitant kind, and seemed to think of it as a basic requirement for an intellectually honest life. Many modern religious thinkers were uncomfortable with Dewey for this reason. Most mid-century liberals seemed to agree with Dewey in this and shared his expectation that the ongoing secularization of thought in modern culture would result in the gradual disappearance of traditional religious institutions. Some of Dewey's followers felt quite militant about that and sought to hasten the day. They conceived of "secular humanism" as a naturalist substitute for religion, and in its name carried on a campaign against the beliefs of traditional religion.[7] This did not help relations between the liberalism of mid-century and thoughtful members of religious communities.

Selznick would have none of this, and would be quick to point out that secularization has not worked out the way many thought it would. The great religious traditions remain and will no doubt continue to be culture-shaping, character-forming institutions in the future. Though a naturalist himself, Selznick has long harbored doubts about pressing its epistemology too far and making an ideology out of it. His main criticism of Dewey's philosophy has been its failure to take seriously the darker and more dangerous side of human life. He is an admirer of the writings of the religious existentialists Martin Buber, Paul Tillich, and Reinhold Niebuhr, which provide a corrective to Dewey's monotonously sunny outlook in this respect.

There are a lot of good reasons for communitarian liberalism, many of them close to hand, but what are the ultimate reasons for a communitarian morality? Why should we honor the principle of moral equality? Religious communities have always insisted that the first responsibility is responsibility to God. As Selznick points out, all the great religious traditions, including Buddhism and Hinduism, would find unconstrained individualism incoherent, even abhorrent, and for this reason they have been the main vessels of communitarian morals throughout history. Evils great and small have been committed in the name of God, but what lesson are we to draw from that insight? Seen from the inside of the great traditions, the ideal of the religious life is the theonomous self. Here autonomy is necessary but not sufficient. There is a search for more, and especially important, Selznick observes, is "sustained self-scrutiny informed by the belief that there is or can be a connection between limited, frail humanity and another realm, somehow beyond space and time,

7. For an evaluation of this humanist movement and its shortcomings from the standpoint of the philosophy of religion, see John E. Smith, *Quasi-Religions: Humanism, Marxism and Nationalism* (New York: St. Martin's Press, 1994). The interplay throughout the course of American history between the influence of Enlightenment values of individual autonomy, democracy, and secularity, on the one hand, and religious traditions of community, authority, and learning, on the other, is explored by prominent scholars in William M. Shea and Peter A. Huff, eds., *Knowledge and Belief in America: Enlightenment Traditions and Modern Religious Thought* (New York: Woodrow Wilson Center Press and Cambridge University Press, 1995).

worthy of reverence, awe, and worship." Religions retain their appeal and their warrant, he suggests, because "they foster self-scrutiny, self-transcendence, loyalty, and humility."

These are essential to the prospects for communitarian liberalism, and whatever secures them in experience and thought is worthy of respectful attention. A new kind of ecumenical moment has arrived in the cultural life of late modernity, Selznick suggests, and it should reach beyond the dialogues of the churches to include secular philosophy and its adherents as well. They share an interest in the experience and evaluation of moral principles, and should have a good deal to talk about. A proper starting point is offered by his conclusion on the interdependence of the twin foundations of the moral order in society, civility and piety: "civility is naked without articles of faith, which tell us who we are and what we live by, and piety without civility is debased and out of control."

Michael J. Lacey

PREFACE

In the 1980s, when I was writing *The Moral Commonwealth,* I came to realize that my arguments were very much in line with the then-emerging communitarian philosophy being articulated by Amitai Etzioni, Charles Taylor, Michael Sandel, and others. I accepted that affiliation, and in the 1990s published essays on various aspects of the communitarian perspective. I was especially keen to show that such a doctrine, properly understood, belongs within the progressive tradition of American political and social thought.

In 1997 I was invited to give the Austin Lecture at the Edinburgh meeting of the United Kingdom Association for Legal and Social Philosophy. My topic was "The Communitarian Persuasion." I am grateful to my hosts for that invitation, for their warm hospitality, and for arranging an extensive and lively discussion. Later that year I participated in a conference on liberalism and communitarianism sponsored by the Research School of Social Science of the Australian National University in Canberra. My contribution was entitled "Communitarian Amendments to the Liberal Project." I appreciated the opportunity to enrich my understanding and refine my views.

The Communitarian Persuasion is a kind of postscript to *The Moral Commonwealth* (Berkeley: University of California Press, 1992). I have taken the liberty of referring the reader to that book for more extended discussion of some topics.

In 1993–94 I was a fellow at the Woodrow Wilson International

Center for Scholars in Washington, D.C. There I met Michael J. Lacey, then director of United States Studies. I appreciated his warm friendship, help, and encouragement. I retained my connection with the Wilson Center as a senior scholar, and Lacey has been a continuing source of ideas and inspiration. Thanks, Mike.

At Berkeley, I received substantial help from the Center for the Study of Law and Society, the Jurisprudence and Social Policy Program in the School of Law, and the university's Committee on Research. I could not have done this work without the able and dedicated assistance of Ryan Cruz Morales and Shalini Satkunanandan. Thanks also to Becky Curry, for helping me get started, and to Rod Watanabe for his never-failing courtesy, help, and good humor.

I am proud and grateful for the advice and friendly criticism offered by many colleagues: Kenneth I. Winston of the John F. Kennedy School of Government at Harvard; my Berkeley colleagues, especially Sanford H. Kadish, Robert Kagan, Ralph Kramer, Sheldon Messinger, Robert Post, and Harry N. Scheiber; also Clare Fischer and Lewis Mudge of the Graduate Theological Union; Carol Heimer of Northwestern University; Joseph Rees of Virginia Polytechnic Institute and State University; Winfried Brugger of Heidelberg University; Hugh Heclo of George Mason University; Wilfred M. McClay of the University of Tennessee at Chattanooga; and Martin Krygier of the University of New South Wales.

A version of chapter 2, "The Idea of Community," is included in *Progressive Politics in the Global Age*, edited by Henry Tam (Cambridge: Polity Press, 2001). I am grateful to Tam for thinking of me, and for making the project a rewarding experience.

Like all who have been touched by the communitarian message, I owe a special debt to Amitai Etzioni for his initiative, his wisdom, and his leadership.

I have dedicated this book to my wife, Doris R. Fine, with love and gratitude.

PS
Berkeley, August 2001

PART ONE

PRECEPTS

A PUBLIC PHILOSOPHY

THE IDEA OF COMMUNITY

AN ETHIC OF RESPONSIBILITY

A UNITY OF UNITIES

CHAPTER I

A PUBLIC PHILOSOPHY

Americans have long embraced and mostly enjoyed the undeniable benefits of modern technology, free enterprise, and liberal democracy. We have been blessed by unprecedented prosperity, less burdensome work, ever widening opportunity, stable government based on the rule of law, and respect for popular will. We have welcomed the waning of male domination and of virulent racism. Real as they are, these achievements are far from complete. Inequality abounds, poverty and prejudice persist, social justice remains a moral imperative.

More is at stake than an unfulfilled dream. Negative forces are at work. A market mentality invades much of social life, undercutting values that need special protection. The pace of change, and widening demands for free choice and expression, erode the authority of parents, and of received tradition. In our liberal democracy it is hard to sustain the difference between liberty and license. Separation of sex and reproduction, sex and marriage, undermines personal responsibility. A remorseless logic of corporate power shifts major decisions to remote places, where accountability is limited or evaded. Modern government is experienced by many as opaque, distant, and oppressive. These and other social trends have generated widespread anxiety and discontent. Everyday life seems out of joint.

Of course, life goes on. Young people connect, love one another, and raise children; the economy hums, more or less vibrantly; many traditions are respected; taxes are collected. However, all is under stress: confidence is shaken even as we require, more than ever, high levels of collective will, energy, discipline, and intelligence.

This diagnosis does not deny the reality of progress. Progressive or not, many modern trends tend to loosen attachments and threaten stability. Under these conditions community—based on interdependence, commitment, and reconciliation—is bound to need healing and restoration. This necessity does not lessen the worth of modern ideals and institutions. But we must think more clearly about them. We cannot protect ideals we do not understand.

THE NEW COMMUNITARIANS

In response to modern and postmodern anxieties, a new voice has emerged, searching for clarity and struggling to be heard. This is the communitarian voice I wish to explain, interpret, and defend.

The label *communitarian* can be applied to any doctrine that prizes collective goods or ideals and limits claims to individual independence and self-realization. The main religious traditions are strongly communitarian in that they demand conformity to divine law, sometimes in excruciating detail. The communist and Nazi movements, and more moderate doctrines of socialism, social democracy, and Christian social thought, may also be called communitarian. Indeed, the quest for a communitarian morality is hardly new. A long list of thinkers—Hegel, Marx, Dewey, and many others, including several popes—have sought alternatives to what seemed to them an impoverished morality and an inadequate understanding of human society. There have been communitarians of left and right: anarchist, socialist, liberal, and conservative. Some of these doctrines and the regimes they created have given the idea of community a very bad name. We would surely want to reject any doctrine that demands supine obedience to tradition or unduly hampers freedom of choice in marriage, work, education, religion, and politics.

The claims of community can indeed go too far. However, all values are threatened when a society falls apart—that is, when it cannot provide its members adequate nurture, support, and coherence. Without *effective* opportunities, the pursuit of happiness is futile and liberty is self-defeating.

In the United States a new communitarian movement emerged

in the early 1980s. This was a response to three important developments. It began as a controversy among philosophers, initiated by Alasdair MacIntyre's *After Virtue* and Michael Sandel's *Liberalism and the Limits of Justice* (both published in 1982). These and other philosophical writings criticized the premises of liberalism, especially political and economic individualism and the notion that people can readily and desirably free themselves from unchosen attachments and obligations. These critics were called "communitarian," and the so-called communitarian-liberal debate quickly became a staple of academic social and moral philosophy. This excitement among professors was doubtless driven in part by the wish to enliven college teaching and by the appeal of polemical exchanges. Nevertheless, something important was going on—the quest for a public philosophy that could take account of what liberalism failed to appreciate as well as what it could clearly see and rightly teach.

A second source of the new communitarianism, more closely tied to political issues, was a response to the Reagan/Thatcher era in the United States and Britain during the 1980s. Those leaders gave full rein to unbridled capitalism, encouraging distrust of government, resistance to taxation, and a strong preference for market solutions to all problems. This mentality, which ignored what Amitai Etzioni called "the moral dimension,"[1] sounded a full retreat from social responsibility.

Third was a growing uneasiness about the welfare state among those who had been its loyal supporters. This disaffection had already been expressed by Robert F. Kennedy when he campaigned for the presidency in 1968. As Michael Sandel recounts:

> RFK's political outlook was in some ways more conservative and in some ways more radical than the mainstream of his party. He worried about the remoteness of big government, favored decentralized power, criticized welfare as "our greatest domestic failure," challenged the faith in economic growth as a panacea for social ills, and took a hard line on crime. . . . Kennedy's clearest difference with mainstream liberal opinion was over welfare. Unlike conservatives, who opposed federal spending for the poor, Kennedy criticized welfare on the grounds

---

1. See Amitai Etzioni, *The Moral Dimension: Toward a New Economics* (New York: Free Press, 1988).

that it made millions of Americans dependent on handouts and thus unable to play a role in the democracy. "Fellowship, community, shared patriotism—these essential values of our civilization do not come from just buying and consuming goods together. They come from a shared sense of interdependence and personal effort."[2]

With these words, Robert Kennedy gave early expression to what would become major themes in contemporary communitarian thought.

In 1996 a leading German Social Democrat offered this confession:

We Social Democrats created an overly regulated, overly bureaucratic and overly professionalized welfare state. We believed, for example, that if the state bore the responsibility for the outcome of a process, it must regulate this process itself. This was a conceptual error. We did not believe in people's capacity for spontaneously helping and caring for others in the neighborhoods; we did not dare to hope that parents of schoolchildren would take care of the upkeep of classrooms; we did not believe that we could leave the running of a kindergarten to the parents. . . . To a certain extent, we succumbed to a blind faith in science and experts.[3]

This was another effort to rethink the moral and political premises of the welfare state.

The new communitarians are well aware that community has dangers and deficits as well as benefits. They have tried to think anew, conscious of the need to vindicate freedom as well as solidarity,

---

2. Michael Sandel, "My RFK," *The New Republic*, July 6, 1998, 11. See also Sandel, *Democracy's Discontents* (Cambridge, Mass.: Harvard University Press, 1996), pp. 299–304. Sandel notes: "Drawing on the voluntarist conception of freedom, many liberals of the day argued that the solution to poverty was welfare, ideally in the form of a guaranteed minimum income that imposed no conditions and made no judgments about the lives recipients led. Respecting persons as free and independent selves, capable of choosing their own ends, meant providing each person as a matter of right a certain measure of economic security. Kennedy disagreed" (p. 302).

3. Rudolf Scharping, "Freedom, Solidarity, Individual Responsibility: Reflections on the Relationship between Politics, Money and Morality," comments prepared for a communitarian conference held in Geneva, Switzerland, August 1996. Scharping became Germany's minister of defense after the Social Democrats won the election in 1998.

rights as well as responsibilities.[4] A central theme is the enhancement of personal and social responsibility. The communitarian ethos is not mainly about sympathy, benevolence, or compassion. It is about meeting our obligations as responsible parents, children, employees, employers, officials, and citizens. These obligations are *eased* by love and *supported* by love. But they arise and persist even when love is absent or hard to sustain.

COMMUNITARIAN LIBERALISM

Are the new communitarians antiliberal? It might seem so, since they have often criticized liberal theory and policy. But they have by no means rejected liberal institutions and the liberal tradition. Rather, the new communitarians have argued that liberal premises are overly individualistic, insufficiently sensitive to the social sources of selfhood and obligation, too much concerned with rights and too little with duty, too ready to accept an anemic conception of the common good. The operative words are *overly, insufficiently, too much, too ready.* Thus the main target of communitarian criticism is intellectual and practical excess. Good ideas are put forward without proper regard for limiting conditions, competing principles, and informing contexts.

The new communitarians accept and support the main liberal achievements. For their part, many contemporary liberals have adopted communitarian perspectives, especially with respect to economic policy, environmental protection, and social justice. Western ideals of freedom, equality, tolerance, and rationality owe much to the work of liberal thinkers and political leaders. However, some of the most important of these ideas are not unique to liberalism. They belong to the heritage of Western civilization, including ideas we associate with Greek, Roman, and Judeo-Christian experience.

Liberalism is a many-stranded tradition, not a well-defined ideology or tight system of premises and conclusions. Even a glance at the history of liberalism shows important differences among, for

---

4. *The Responsive Community,* edited by Amitai Etzioni, journal of the new communitarians, carries the subtitle "Rights *and* Responsibilities." The editorial board includes, among others, Benjamin R. Barber, Robert N. Bellah, Jean Bethke Elshtain, William Galston, Nathan Glazer, Mary Ann Glendon, and Charles Taylor.

example, Locke, Rousseau, Mill, and Dewey. Most revealing is the transition from "classical" or "market" liberalism to "welfare" liberalism. The great liberal thinkers of the seventeenth and eighteenth centuries, such as John Locke and Adam Smith, sought freedom from ignorance, dogma, despotism, and privilege; they helped break the hold of a feudal, clerical, and mercantilist past. In doing so they laid foundations for democracy, the rule of law, and free enterprise. These great achievements were marred, however, by a basic flaw. Their chief targets were (and in the historical context had to be) arbitrary government and class privilege. They wanted justice, but this meant mainly *formal* justice. As Anatole France put it, in a memorable passage, "the law, in its majestic equality, forbids the rich as well as the poor to sleep under bridges, beg in the streets, and steal bread."[5]

This crippling condition was widely recognized in the nineteenth century. As the social costs of the Industrial Revolution were made plain, new demands were heard for a fuller measure of freedom, equality, and justice. Many liberals came to see that people cannot enjoy freedom if they are poor and ignorant; cannot receive justice if their circumstances are ignored; cannot be rational if they believe they must submit to unquestioned authority; cannot be citizens of a democracy if they are barred from joining with others to pursue their interests and claim their rights.

Even John Stuart Mill, in many ways the quintessential nineteenth-century liberal, came to reject economic individualism in favor of a more cooperative, more caring, more just society.[6] Other English "new liberals" supported active interventions by government to expand opportunity and regulate markets. Since Franklin D. Roosevelt's New Deal, American liberals have embraced welfare liberalism, leaving market liberalism to become the intellectual property of American conservatism. For welfare liberals, democratic government is not an enemy of freedom. So long as constitutional safeguards are in place, government can and should have a major role in defining and achieving the common good.

Welfare liberals share many communitarian ideas. They have

5. The quotation is more famous than its source: Anatole France, *The Red Lily*, trans. Winfred Stephens (London: John Lane, 1914), p. 95.
6. See *Autobiography of John Stuart Mill* (1873; reprint, New York: Columbia University Press, 1924), p. 162.

criticized economic individualism, especially the view that the free play of private interests will necessarily serve the general welfare. Welfare liberalism's concern for the poor, and for disadvantaged minorities, is an expression of fraternity. These are communitarian sensibilities. However, important differences separate the new communitarians from welfare liberals. The latter have been overly complacent with respect to major social problems, such as widespread dependency on public assistance; premature pregnancies and fatherless children; unsafe neighborhoods, schools, parks, and other public spaces; erosion of support for traditional conceptions of good conduct and personal responsibility.

The new communitarians reject welfare-state programs that are overly bureaucratic or based on misconceptions about what people in poverty are like. They want to remedy past failures through policies that encourage personal responsibility on the part of clients, in health care and other social services, and more effective participation by local governments, concerned citizens, and private institutions.

The new communitarians also believe that American liberalism has gone too far in pressing demands for political liberty and personal autonomy. In the nineteenth and early twentieth centuries, liberals could speak comfortably about "ordered liberty," but that phrase has been retired. A fateful step was the distinction drawn by welfare liberals, beginning in the 1930s, between economic and political liberty. The New Deal introduced many restraints on business, rejected "freedom of contract" as a constitutional bar to laws protecting factory workers, and created a wide array of regulatory agencies to police finance, industry, and agriculture. At the same time, American liberals ardently supported civil rights and civil liberties. For them, First Amendment rights have special primacy. Rights of free speech and expression are sacred, to be vigorously defended against encroachment or erosion. This defense of freedom deserves the gratitude of all Americans. Yet the community is disarmed by liberal ideas that rationalize or excuse irresponsible conduct. A new balance is required, based on a better understanding of ordered liberty.

Too many contemporary American liberals have accepted a radical relativism whose message is that all values are subjective and of equal worth. Such ideas have undercut confidence in moral judgment and democratic decision. Closely related is the doctrine of liberal neutralism, the idea that government should not presume to say what sort of lives we ought to live and should not try to mold our preferences. According to this liberal view, moral judgments are properly made by individuals and not by communities, not even by democratic communities. An underlying assumption is that differences about values run deep and cannot be reconciled. Hence government should leave them alone. As we shall see, this is very different from the communitarian understanding of democracy.

American welfare liberalism has had a split personality. It has rejected the individualist assumptions of neoclassical economics about property and choice. Welfare liberals accept many government policies that limit free choice in matters of health, safety, education, and conservation. American liberals are not consistently libertarian. Although they are fervent defenders of civil liberties and civil rights, they do not shrink from asking people to give up riding bicycles without helmets or purchasing handguns without restrictions. They mostly favor public education, public television, government support for the arts, and regulation of spending in political campaigns. The troubled ethos of welfare liberalism badly needs a forthright acceptance of communitarian principles. This will produce a sturdy hybrid, which we may call communitarian liberalism.

The communitarian critique of liberalism has this main complaint: the liberal tradition as we have come to know it in the West lacks an ethic of responsibility. The focus has been on liberty and rights, without much concern for obligation and duty. This failing is easy to understand and even forgive. Modern liberalism emerged as an appeal for liberation from the shackles of a precapitalist and predemocratic age. Liberals fought for an end to class privilege, fixed status, suffocating tradition, and outmoded institutions. The guiding lights would be autonomy and choice. The sobering virtues of responsibility were given little weight, or were taken for granted.

The communitarian challenge seeks to amend liberalism, not to reject it. There is no question of idealizing, still less of returning to, a world of protected privilege; no question of giving up the chief economic, political, and social liberties championed by the architects of liberal government. Nevertheless, the communitarian amendments are not minor, and they claim coherence. The message is one of solidarity repaired, and of liberty protected by well-ordered institutions and norms of civility. In prospect is an alternative vision of human persons as free in vital respects but limited by duties that make those freedoms effective and secure.

KINDRED VOICES

The new communitarians can make no claim to originality, or to ideological purity. Like most Americans, they accept a great part of the
liberal tradition. Like most Americans, they accept other ideas as well.
Following is a short description of kindred voices within the broad
spectrum of what I have called communitarian liberalism.[7]

Strands of Conservatism. In authentic conservatism,[8] the keynote is
personal, cultural, and institutional security. These goals require a
well-knit social life. The new communitarians share conservative
concerns for cultural continuity, for restraint in the pursuit of self-
interest, and for threshold moral standards to which all must adhere.
However, communitarians are more aware of the evils that come
from unexamined adherence to outmoded ideas. Although traditions
deserve respect, they should be open to change in the light of new
circumstances, new knowledge, and competing values.

Conservatives worry about institutions, especially when they are
vulnerable to the corrosive pressures of a market economy and populist democracy. Communitarians recognize and resist such pressures,
yet insist that institutions should be responsive. Responsive institutions defend their distinctive values and missions, yet are open to
voices and interests hitherto unheard or disregarded. Responsive
institutions are not rigid or complacent. They are nourished by criticism as well as by trust.

Conservatives and communitarians share a preference for self-
regulation rather than "command and control." Both care about the
vitality of nongovernmental associations and institutions. Communitarians are perhaps more deeply conservative in that they believe
government can and should be an integral part of the community,
neither above nor opposed to it.

The conservative strand is most apparent in a shared preoccupation with the idea of community. Conservative writers have brought
that idea to the fore, honoring its claims, drawing inspiration from
its promise.[9] However, the new communitarians do not share the
nineteenth-century conservatives' hostility to modernity, nor do they

7. For more on this background, see Michael J. Lacey's foreword to this book.
8. Not to be confused with laissez-faire or market liberalism, which has become
the centerpiece of contemporary American conservatism.
9. See Robert A. Nisbet, *The Quest for Community* (New York: Oxford University
Press, 1953).

accept the contemporary conservatives' indifference to social justice, their flight from collective responsibility, and their inclination to defend the status quo rather than seek new ways of dealing with society's problems.

Echoes of Socialism. Although they firmly reject Marxism and Leninism, communitarians share some socialist ideas. Many contemporary "democratic socialists" cling to a socialist identity because they believe the core of socialism is a moral ideal, a vision that transcends the failed strategies and policies of earlier generations. At bottom, they believe, socialism is a quest for social justice, which means, above all, unflagging concern for those who have gained least from modern prosperity, education, and democracy. Social justice takes seriously the rightful claims of all persons to life, health, dignity, and hope.

Judeo-Christian Ethics. The communitarian vision has much in common with major themes in the Old and New Testaments. The Hebrew prophets were fervent advocates of social justice. In Christian doctrine these messages received new authority, and a new idiom. Actually existing religious communities have been notoriously insular and defiled by bigotry. Yet the same traditions have done much to elevate moral sensibilities. Two modern examples are Roman Catholic social teachings and the Protestant social gospel. In the nineteenth and twentieth centuries several papal encyclicals called for moral restraints on economic and political individualism. Popes Leo XIII and Pius XI criticized child labor and bad working conditions. They also defended the right of workers to form trade unions. These ideas helped create a significant "Catholic worker" movement in the United States and, in Europe, Christian socialist political parties. The Second Vatican Council (1962–65) made many changes in Catholic liturgy and doctrine, promising a new era of self-scrutiny and openness. Another milestone was the pastoral letter on economic justice published by the American Catholic bishops in 1986. The bishops spoke loudly for social justice, including a "preferential option for the poor."

The social gospel, which became prominent among American Protestants in the early years of the twentieth century, reaffirmed the biblical teachings on social justice. This movement helped give shape (and leadership) to American socialism, thus distinguishing it from Marxist and communist ideologies.

For the most part, these religious initiatives have been liberal as

well as communitarian. They have supported constitutional democracy, including political and religious pluralism. Among Roman
Catholics, a big step in that direction was taken when church leaders
abandoned the view that God speaks with a single voice, and that
theological error has no rights.[10]

New Liberalisms. Earlier I mentioned recurrent efforts to modify
that "classical" liberalism of individualism and laissez-faire which
became liberal orthodoxy in the nineteenth century. Among classical liberals the prevalence of poverty was not a big concern, nor were
other barriers to full participation in political and economic life. In
the late nineteenth century, seeking to correct these moral deficits,
new liberals in England championed political reform and social justice. Similar views were expressed, in more emphatic ways, during
the Progressive Era in the United States, reflected in the policies of
Presidents Theodore Roosevelt and Woodrow Wilson. New liberalism
in America came of age during President Franklin D. Roosevelt's
New Deal. Although the New Deal liberals were reformers, they had
no basic quarrel with the political system or with capitalist enterprise. They wanted to create a vigorous, problem-solving democracy.
They thought it was wise to regulate self-interest for the common
good.

During the 1920s and 1930s the moral and social philosophy of
American pragmatism was a strong voice on behalf of new liberalism. John Dewey's writings were especially influential in providing
intellectual foundations for communitarian liberalism. Dewey prized
individuality but rejected individualism, especially economic individualism. He stressed the realities of interdependence, the virtues
of cooperation, and the obligations that attend responsible choice.
He combined a spirit of liberation with a strong commitment to effective, self-preserving participation in community life. Dewey gave
paramount importance to the moral and intellectual growth of children. In his proposals for progressive education he advocated treating
schools as communities, and making them more integral parts of their
surrounding communities.

---

10. Catholic responses to modernity, especially Enlightenment ideas and the
French Revolution, were sometimes very conservative and traditionalist, sometimes
more sensitive to the plight of labor and the limits of opportunity. See John A. Coleman, "Neither Liberal nor Socialist," in *One Hundred Years of Catholic Social
Thought*, ed. John A. Coleman (Maryknoll, N.Y.: Orbis Books, 1991), pp. 25–42.

Dewey thought democracy should be a way of life as well as a form of government. Democratic communities discern the common good by exercising collective intelligence, nurtured and refined by rational deliberation, planning, and experiment. He thought art, education, and science were not the preserve of elites, but belonged to everyone. Because of these views Dewey has been called the philosopher of the common man. This American version of new liberalism is still the best intellectual foundation for a public philosophy that speaks to the needs and challenges of our time.[11]

WITHOUT VISION, THE PEOPLE PERISH

The communitarian persuasion is a public philosophy, not a hardened ideology. This is an important distinction to maintain when we consider the role of ideas in public affairs. We cannot do without comprehensive doctrines. They are indispensable as guides to social policy and as foundations of our institutions. They express the sense we make of social reality and the grasp we have of moral truth. For communitarians the compelling reality is human interdependence. The important truth is a pervasive need for personal and social responsibility.

Without a coherent public philosophy we are vulnerable to drift, opportunism, and self-deception. A moral compass is lost or broken. This insight is captured by the biblical aphorism, "where there is no vision, the people perish" (Prov. 29:18).

Americans are rightly distrustful of ideology. The "-isms" of our time, and of earlier times as well, have too often demanded conformity, enforced exclusions, justified murder. Sectarian passions have poisoned Christianity, Marxism, and many other religious and secular movements. Prizing purity of doctrine and unconditional be-

---

11. At a philosophical level Dewey's affinity with communitarian thought is shown by his appreciation for the constructive continuities of social, personal, and intellectual life. He rejected "pernicious dualisms," such as the oppositions of individual and society, ideals and realities, learning and doing, science and common sense, means and ends. Boundaries should be permeable, open to communication and mutual influence. Dewey's "naturalism" embraced ideals as well as their enabling and limiting conditions, and he located ideals, including morality, in the problem-solving experience of everyday life. Dewey welcomed diversity, but did so without giving up or weakening the idea of a common humanity.

lief, these ideologies have often imposed stringent tests of adherence and loyalty. They have expected their beliefs to provide ready answers to all problems. Ideological thinking, it has been said, moves from thought to action "as the crow flies," unimpeded by the rough terrain of competing interests and contradictory values.[12]

Of course, a public philosophy must have some bite, promoting its own perspectives, as when Republicans in the United States seek to curb the role of government in economic and social life. It degenerates into a hardened ideology when adherents become participants in partisan combat rather than deliberative inquiry and when ideological preferences are given free rein, unchecked by concern for other interests or social reality. A true public philosophy is problem-centered: it deals with issues on their merits, in the light of relevant facts and genuine needs. Its principles are tested by their usefulness in promoting good policy. A public philosophy cannot be true to itself and also be a device for escaping the complexities and burdens of choice. When President Lincoln spoke of "firmness in the right as God gives us to see the right," he was not seeking a license for arrogance, still less for complacency or partisan judgment. He was defending principled judgment, tempered by humility, disciplined by self-correction.

12. Michael Oakeshott, *Rationalism in Politics* (New York: Basic Books, 1962), p. 69.

CHAPTER 2

THE IDEA OF COMMUNITY

For many thoughtful people, "community" is a very troublesome idea—frustratingly vague, elusive, even dangerous. These concerns are not frivolous, but they apply at least as much to many other key ideas in philosophy and social science, notably "morality," "law," "culture," "freedom," and "rationality." All have contested meanings; all give cover to undesirable policies and arbitrary power. Yet each has rich and wholesome connotations as well, which have preoccupied scholars for many centuries. "Community" is no exception. We need to clarify the idea, disentangle its elements, and explore its relevance for contemporary thought. We look for guidance to the whole experience of community, its dangers and deficits as well as its virtues.

As a starting point, it is useful to distinguish communities from special-purpose organizations, such as business firms, government agencies, military units, or interest groups. A special-purpose organization may become a community, or something like a community, but its main point is to muster human energies in disciplined ways for particular ends. As "rational systems," organizations strive for efficiency and effectiveness. In contrast, communities are frameworks within which people pursue many different purposes. In communities people share a common life. They are governed, but they are not managed or commanded. In a business or an army, employees or soldiers are "human resources." We do not apply that idiom to communities, except perhaps in wartime, when "mobilization" is the keynote.

THE PRINCIPLE OF COMMUNITY

When we appeal to community as a guiding ideal, we have in mind the moral bonds of membership and leadership. These are the obligations people owe to one another and to the whole of which they are parts. Bonds of community arise from interdependence and from an awareness of shared identity. They are peculiar in that they protect as well as demand. People are not mere means or resources, to be deployed, manipulated, or sacrificed without concern for their interests as individuals. Here we discern the animating principle of community, which we may call "the union of solidarity and respect."

This principle has great practical significance. It comes into play wherever the quality of human relations is important, wherever more than minimal levels of morale and performance are desired. In business or military organizations many efforts are made to approximate (or sometimes fake) the principle of community.[1] This is because employees and soldiers accept discipline more readily, do their jobs better, and cooperate more effectively when they are treated with respect, when their connections are personal as well as goal-directed, when they feel protected and nurtured as well as controlled, and when they feel included as valued members of an enterprise, which both requires and gives loyalty.

So community is about respect and nurture as well as solidarity. Solidarity then takes on a special character and is subject to moral judgment. Divorced from caring, solidarity is more likely to be a caricature of community than a fair representation of its meaning and promise. To give up personal dignity and integrity in exchange for pay, or for the satisfaction of serving a leader or cause, is a distortion of community, not a fulfillment of it.

The moral bonds of community are much like those of friendship and family. These attachments also show the union of solidarity

---

1. It has often been noted that business firms and other organizations try to create a sense of community without providing for the reality of community. But this should remind us of the adage that "hypocrisy is the homage which vice renders to virtue."

and respect. People strike a balance between the needs they have as individual persons and what they owe to one another. In a good friendship, marriage, or family, people readily grant the freedoms respect requires. We have no trouble understanding that excessive control and inappropriate dependency are pathological states. These judgments do not move us to reject the ideal or to think of it as unattainable.

In one important respect, however, community differs from family and friendship. Families and friendships create special bonds that set people apart. In contrast, the experience of community draws us outward as well as inward, toward inclusion as well as exclusion. Although communities build on the limited and intimate associations of kinship, acquaintance, and locality, they beckon us to farther horizons and broader loyalties.

Diversity and inclusion are no strangers to community. In many contexts we understand community as made up of relatively loosely coordinated activities and groups. Thus the "Catholic community" includes all communicants, lay and clerical, as well as a variety of schools, monastic orders, publishers, and sports teams. Loyalty and cohesion are certainly important, but so is an implied promise of caring and concern for everyone's interests. Much the same may be said of expressions like "the university community," "the law school community," "the medical community," "the intelligence community." Inclusion is the leitmotif: in colleges, staff and students as well as professors; in government, a cluster of cooperating agencies. For the sake of community, boundaries are broken down. The focus shifts to a common enterprise and a common life.

THE EXPERIENCE OF COMMUNITY

What makes for community is a very practical question that must be faced by anyone who wants to improve the quality and effectiveness of group life. Although most communities develop without plan, many are consciously designed and carefully nurtured. In such cases leaders or organizers have to know how communities develop and what makes them strong or weak. Even ordinary communities, based on friendship and kinship, may need attention and repair. The everyday life of a school or a business may do little to enhance and much to undermine communication, initiative, and willingness to achieve. Communities take work to create and more work to sustain. With good luck and enough time the process may seem natural, as if foresight and dedication were unimportant. But flourishing communities need a lot of support, including specialized institutions such as government and education, as well as people who can be custodians and physicians of community. We call them parents, teachers, pastors, judges, and leaders.

The main bonds of community are well known. I mention them only briefly, by way of reminder. Most obvious, and often most important, is a shared history or "community of memory."[2] A shared history may point with pride or anguish to sacred origins, acute suffering, or glorious victories. It may also be more homely and modest, such as family pictures in a treasured album. Splendid or modest, sacred or mundane, a shared history needs reminders: anniversaries, anecdotes, orations, legends. In these ways memory is touched up and identities are formed.

A community's memory is the font of shared beliefs, thought-ways, and rules for right conduct. This is, for the most part, a world taken for granted, accepted unconsciously in the course of growing up and as a result of unquestioned practice. However, rules and beliefs are not equally compelling. Some are fully internalized and strictly observed; others are frequently evaded, ignored, misunderstood, or self-interestedly misconstrued. People accept some obligations uncritically, while others are closely scrutinized and often challenged. Some rules are quite specific about what they require, many are ambiguous and open to interpretation. Thus the "normative order" is no solid cake of custom. Even in relatively stable and apparently simple societies, we find lively controversy and subtle argument.

Something more is wanted than a "sense" of community. Communities are sustained by the realities of everyday life, including interdependence, reciprocity, and self-interest. If people do not need each other, if little is to be gained from participation and commitment, communities are not likely to emerge or endure. This practical and

2. Robert N. Bellah et al., *Habits of the Heart: Individualism and Commitment in American Life* (Berkeley: University of California Press, 1985), pp. 152–155.

rational element is often overlooked by theorists. It is not news to anyone who has had hands-on experience in community organization. Self-interest is not necessarily an enemy of community. It is, on the contrary, an engine of community, a reliable basis for cooperation and commitment. This is no disparagement of friendship, love, or loyalty. However, love and reciprocity need each other; they wither when apart.

Communities are strengthened when belonging takes many forms, when members are animated by diverse and compelling motives, and when they can further their varied interests within the framework of a particular community. Even within religious or ethnic communities, where shared identities are so important, solidarity is enhanced by opportunities for child care, education, recreation, charity, and self-improvement. Similarly, social or political movements often look to a rich internal life for cohesion and morale. Communities are weakened when social life is fragmented—that is, when work, family, residence, religion, education, and politics are unconnected or at odds. Without a common life—without overlapping interests and different ways of belonging—the bonds of community are weak and vulnerable.

A common life is furthered when boundaries are blurred—for example, between parenting and teaching, work and recreation, religion and social work. The experience of community is strengthened when these activities reinforce one another. The autonomy of institutions need not be lost. But where boundaries are blurred, people's lives and activities intersect and overlap in supportive ways.

NOT ALL OR NONE

A simple but essential conclusion can be drawn from the sociology of community. Groups are more or less full-blown communities, and they can be communities in different ways. Some arise mainly from kinship and locality, others from shared ideals or a common enterprise. With this conclusion in mind, we may define community as follows: A group is a community *insofar as* it embraces a wide range of interests and activities; *insofar as* it takes account of whole persons, not just specialized contributions or roles; and *insofar as* bonds of commitment and culture are shared.

These conditions shift attention from the question, "is this a community?" toward the question "how far and in what ways does this group experience the bonds, benefits, and deficits of community?" By attending to this variability we can focus on the difficult and uneven process of building or strengthening communities. Most important, we can more readily recognize that the values we associate with community can be sought, with different strategies and varying success, wherever sustained human interaction takes place—in family life, work, education, politics, health care, urban design. In each sphere we can find ways of encouraging responsible conduct; we can enlarge opportunities for mutual caring and concern; we can find the right recipe for achieving a union of solidarity and respect.

KINDS AND CONTEXTS

In some communities a shared history is crucial; others make the most of a religious or political identity. In addition, all communities have rules—but, as I have already pointed out, rules are not equally sacred, nor do they necessarily spell out in great detail what people must do. These differences remind us that communities vary in kind, as well as in the extent to which communal bonds exist. Monastic communities are closely controlled and turn life inward. Professional or occupational communities—police, military, legal, medical—are unified by craft values or by a distinctive style of life. Communities based on extended families and common ancestry are held together by inheritance, family traditions, patronage, and other special claims and obligations. In short, communities have different ways of bonding.

It is sometimes thought that the most tightly knit community is also the most genuine or ideal community. That is a mistake. A very tightly knit community is likely to be distorted in one way or another, perhaps overly exclusive and withdrawn, or demanding too much commitment and conformity. Some such communities—religious or therapeutic—have special needs, and are recognized as special by the larger community within which they exist as isolated and perhaps protected enclaves. Natural communities are less disciplined, less insistent on conformity. They are not governed by a closely specified ideal, such as a monastic way of life; they are more likely to result from unplanned adaptation, sustained by the need for order and by the benefits of cooperation. Normal communities take account of how people actually live, and want to live, not only how we would like them to live.[3]

The features of a normal community are suggested in the following account of "hippie" enclaves in the 1960s:

> Typically, communes were made up fairly uniformly of young people who identified with the hip subculture of drugs, rock and voluntary poverty. . . . By contrast, the community embraced a greater diversity of people, not just the hip and the young. Where communes left finances, work and decision to the fickle will of group consciousness, communities leaned more heavily on definite structures: work systems, treasurers, and corporations. . . . The physical, as well as emotional, distance was greater in a community than in a commune. Traditionally, a community was made up of separate houses rather than a large common dwelling.[4]

The commune seeks communion, not community; psychic unity, not the harmony and discord of ordinary life.

Scientific Communities. In his writings on the history of science, Thomas Kuhn showed how good science depends on shared standards and ways of thinking.[5] These include basic requirements of a scientific attitude, such as accuracy and objectivity, and more specific criteria of respectable and creative work in a particular discipline, such as geology, physics, or chemistry. Each discipline is governed by norms of argument and evidence, including mathematical arguments, and by other criteria of good science, such as what knowledge should be taken as settled, at least for the inquiry at hand. Transmitted in the course of scientific education, these standards are reinforced when new professors and research scientists are appointed, and in the course of peer review of applications for research grants.

As in other communities, the norms of science create personal

---

3. On the distinctive characteristics of a tightly knit community, see Benjamin Zablocki, *The Joyful Community* (Baltimore: Penguin Books, 1971).

4. Robert Houriet, *Getting Back Together* (New York: Coward-McCann, 1971), pp. 205–206.

5. *The Structure of Scientific Revolutions* (Chicago: University of Chicago Press, 1970). For more on Kuhn and subjectivity, see *The Moral Commonwealth* (Berkeley: University of California Press, 1992), pp. 82–88.

and group identities. They say what it means to be a self-respecting physicist or entomologist. But what Kuhn calls the "disciplinary matrix"—the special premises and rules of a particular science—is only incidentally about identity. It is mainly about the benefits of community for creativity, productivity, and excellence. The ethos of science encourages initiative, challenge, and dissent, but the challenge must be credible, the dissent responsible.

There are many sciences and kinds of science. Nevertheless, common threads exist. All sciences demand empirical research and theoretical explanation. All foster respect for contingency, sensitivity to variation, and a spirit of self-correction. These ideals are not always fulfilled; standards are not always met. They are alive and well, however, wherever good science is pursued, offering inspiration and guidance, telling us how to distinguish science from pseudoscience.

Behind the Diversity. In studying kinds of community, we have to know what each kind requires, what each has to offer, and what sacrifices each demands. Yet essential features of community remain. If we keep those features in mind, we can consider the benefits and costs of community in the context at hand. In scientific communities, for example, we can examine the benefits and costs of sharing a common perspective.[6] We can learn how to create or repair a particular kind of community. To do so, however, we must understand what makes for commuity, what enhances community, and what undermines it. We would not want to create a counterfeit community, or a parody of community. If we want a special kind of community, such as a democratic community, a religious community, or a community of scientists or scholars, we should have reason to believe it is a *community* we are creating and not something else.

VIRTUES AND DEFICITS

There is nothing unusual about the coexistence and interdependence of good and evil. We can safely say, with little exaggeration, that every

---

6. A distinctive perspective has great benefits for the education of new scholars and scientists, but it may also create an undesirable orthodoxy and serve to insulate the discipline from other disciplines.

virtue has a humbling vice. Hence, we often need to defend "genuine" love, freedom, friendship, religion, democracy, law, education, or science from distortions or corruptions, many of which stem from their own weaknesses and temptations. Love may create emotional dependency; religion is corrupted by superstition, science by mindless scientism, democracy by populist excess, journalism by pressures to make news entertaining. Being aware of these dangers does not lead us to spurn love or reject science. Instead, we try to discover what is genuine and how to achieve it.

Like family, friendship, knowledge, and statesmanship, community is a prima facie good. This favorable presumption is justified by what we have learned from much experience. The presumption is rebuttable, however, by showing that, in a particular case, the evil outweighs the good or must be cured if the good is to survive. A community may be distracted and crippled by ideological extremism, or by corrupt or criminal activity.

The prime virtue of community is an ethos of open-ended obligation. An obligation is open-ended when it endures despite many changes in circumstance and expectation, and when it may expand or contract in response to those changes. Marriages are supposed to last through good times and bad, "for richer or poorer, in sickness or health." Parents have open-ended obligations to their children, and children to their parents. In these relationships people often make choices—whether and whom to marry, whether to have children, and how many—but once the commitment has been made, choice fades in importance. Parents must care for the children they have, not for those they would like to have had, and children have the same obligations toward the elderly parents they actually have.

The principle of open-ended obligation applies well beyond marriage and parenting. It has force wherever caring and commitment matter. It has the effect of enlarging the obligations fixed by contract or by the apparent limits of professional responsibility. Open-ended obligations arise in many settings: among employers and employees, teachers and students, doctors and patients. Wherever such obligations prevail, people are treated as whole persons, unique and multifaceted, as members of a community. The experience of belonging is thereby enriched.

There is, of course, a downside to this virtue. When obligations are diffuse and unclear, too much may be asked of us, as many family dramas reveal, and as is also revealed in the demands of organizational, political, and professional life.[7] That there are greedy institutions does not mean we should disparage the worth of open-ended obligation, or the settings within which it is wholesome and appropriate. Instead we narrow obligations when that makes more sense. We do not need caring and commitment all the time, nor do we have to find them everywhere. We should look for nurture in a proper place.

The weakening of community in modern times is partly due to the allure and ascendancy of limited obligation. The liberal tradition has celebrated freedom of contract, thereby advancing economic prosperity as well as ideals of choice, dignity, consent, and rationality. In the modern contract terms are specific and the cost of a breach is known. A preference for defined and limited commitments is wholly opposed to the ethos of open-ended obligation.

The idea of contract works best when relationships are temporary or can be readily changed. It makes less sense when continuing relationships are contemplated or required. In much of business or family life, people want to stay connected; they want to retain the benefits of cooperation, despite changing circumstances. Therefore they try to resolve problems by negotiation, without necessarily insisting on the hitherto agreed-to terms.[8] As cooperation takes root, as the experience of community thickens, the principle of limited obligation loses force. It is pushed into the background, invoked only when a breakdown is expected or desired.

Open-ended obligation fosters trust and encourages communication. Trust means people can rely on one another to honor their commitments as parents, friends, or business associates; they can appeal to shared purposes instead of demanding compliance; they can live by the taken-for-granted understandings that underlie a promise or policy. The transition is from arms-length bargaining to a spirit of consultation and joint problem solving.

Trust is the indispensable cement of group life. It is a resource people can draw on when they need help or when they form new families, enterprises, or institutions. Like love and friendship, trust can be misplaced or self-destructive; therefore, it is only a prima facie

---

7. On the demands of organizations, see William H. Whyte Jr., *The Organization Man* (New York: Simon and Schuster, 1956); also Lewis A. Coser, *Greedy Institutions* (New York: Free Press, 1974).

8. Stewart Macaulay, "Non-Contractual Relations in Business: A Preliminary Study," *American Sociological Review* 28 (1963): 61.

good. Moreover, trust creates special claims, vested interests, inertia, and resistance to change. Despite these drawbacks, hardly anyone would deny that people and institutions benefit from trusting others and being trusted.

A less well-understood virtue of community is the contribution it makes to responsible judgment. To participate in community is to be aware of and responsive to a complex set of interests and values. Therefore, the goals we seek and the ideals we embrace are tempered by concern for their effect on other goals and values. Artists, businesspeople, scholars, or politicians cannot be wholly or single-mindedly devoted to their specialized concerns. The more sensitive they are to the communities they belong to, the less free they are to act in wholly self-serving ways. To pursue one's own demon, or one's own ambition, without thought for others, is a kind of irresponsibility. Furthermore, participation in communities is not normally irrational or self-destructive. On the contrary, without the restraints of community, rationality is often precarious and may be lost. An electorate made up of detached individuals, without anchors of interest and association, is vulnerable to manipulation by political demagogues. Young people gain in rationality as they settle down, accept obligations, and choose goals that are genuinely satisfying and attainable. We make self-preserving life plans and rational choices in and through the stable friendships we make, the education we get, the groups and institutions we embrace.

Of course, the experience of belonging can also undermine rationality by limiting horizons, stifling initiative, and fostering uncritical attitudes toward tradition and authority. Here again, the virtue has a humbling vice; here again, the virtue is genuine, despite the vice.

AN IRREPRESSIBLE TENSION

It is obvious that community is not a comfortable idea, blessed with simplicity. On the contrary, it is one of those great concepts from which we learn the perplexities and burdens of social life. Most important is the conflict between exclusion and inclusion. We have good reason to make communities open or permeable in some ways, even if they are closed in other ways. The benefits gained from local attachments are often offset by the advantages people see in broader identities and ideals. This contrast is pervasive and irrepressible, but the conflict is not irreconcilable. Finding ways of accommodating the abiding values of "particularism" and the just claims of "universalism" is a major part of the communitarian project.[9]

9. We revisit the tension between universalist and particularist ways of choosing, judging, and relating in chapter 4, p. 45.

CHAPTER 3

AN ETHIC
OF RESPONSIBILITY

I noted in chapter 1 that the central communitarian message is a call for the enhancement of personal and social responsibility. This emphasis reflects a deep concern for overcoming the negative, community-destroying effects of American individualism. Although our most compelling responsibilities are to other persons, we also owe responsibility to ideals, institutions, and the community as a whole. In the following chapters, dealing with the social fabric, rights, democracy, business enterprise, and social justice, we examine what responsibility means and what principles its achievement requires. Principles of responsibility must be tailored to the context—that is, to the special purposes, tradeoffs, strengths, and vulnerabilities of democracy, education, or family life. An ethic of responsibility cannot by itself provide definitive answers to policy questions. Instead, the ethic inclines us toward strategies of reconciliation, solidarity, and inclusiveness. For example, communitarians are likely to encourage some forms of required community service. However, every such proposal must be assessed in the light of costs, benefits, and competing values. These judgments leave plenty of room for communitarians to disagree about particular policies or programs.

In this chapter we trace responsible conduct to its foundations in human psychology, judgment, and perception. We learn that responsibility is created and enriched, or crippled and killed, by how we perceive ourselves and relate to others. Therefore, we cannot divorce choice from duty. We are responsible for what we choose, and for acting responsibly when we have made a choice. To take responsibility seriously, we must look closely at how we live and work. The duties of parents, teachers, or physicians cannot be known without also knowing the circumstances they must live with and the resources they have. As these facts change, so do responsibilities.[1]

BEYOND ACCOUNTABILITY

When people are asked to follow rules or achieve goals, responsibility has a fairly definite meaning. We think people should be "accountable" for their acts or failures; they should be held responsible. For this we need standards by which to judge conduct and performance, and to determine who is exempt or may be excused. Holding people accountable works best when we can identify threshold criteria of good conduct or performance, as when we ask whether people obey the law or pass a test. Accountability is important, but by itself it is not enough to create an ethic of responsibility.

A broader view of responsibility takes us beyond accountability. The question is not what actions will put you in prison, cost you money, or cause you to lose a professional license. It is, rather, whether and how much you care about your duties. An ethic of responsibility calls for reflection and understanding, not mechanical or bare conformity. It looks to ideals as well as obligations, to values as well as rules.

1. Consider the practice (reported in the *New York Times*, March 21, 1999) of using brand-name products and their familiar logos in mathematics texts for children. Pupils are asked to study the diameters of Oreo cookies, and how long it would take to save up for a pair of Nike shoes. These "real world" examples are supposed to make math more relevant to sixth-graders. (Eager to cooperate, the manufacturers offer the use of their logos without charge.) This practice has been criticized as rank commercialism, and indeed it is a questionable idea to stimulate demand for sugary cookies and modish shoes. A deeper concern, however, is the thoughtful choice of exercises and examples, which, by teaching more than math, can encourage better ways of being a consumer, staying healthy, taking turns, and sharing possessions. Responsible teaching is not achieved by single-minded preoccupation with particular subjects or skills.

An ordinary pedestrian does not have to do much more than obey signals and avoid jaywalking; customers pay for what they take or consume. In either case, however, being truly responsible means being guided by duty, and by concern for others, not by worries about legal penalties.

As obligations and relationships intensify—as they become more enduring and more complex—following rules is not enough. A responsible employee shows initiative as well as conformity; responsible lovers consider the physical and emotional well-being of their partners; responsible citizens study the issues before they vote.

Clear rules are more important for accountability than for a higher ideal of responsible conduct. As American parents know very well, what parenting requires is often uncertain, subject to change, and much affected by circumstances. Obligations are met in the light of what parents and children *can* do as well as what they *should* do. Although rules abound in a tightly run organization, an ethic of responsibility is seldom irrelevant, or unneeded. This is true even or perhaps especially in military units. On maneuvers or in combat more is wanted than following rules.

The responsible person asks: who am I? what is my duty? what does this situation require? These questions presume commitment— to an ideal, a profession, a family, a skill, an institution. The answers reveal an intimate connection between responsibility and community. Responsibility is the psychic tissue of community. Acting responsibly makes for a life enriched by belonging and enhanced by obligation.

Because responsibility requires judgment, it also calls for a measure of autonomy. We say people in authority should be governed by law and answerable to law. Yet we know that rules should be applied with wisdom, taking account of exceptional circumstances, the costs of demanding strict compliance, and the reason behind the rule (that is, what purpose it is supposed to accomplish). Therefore, we give officials room to use good judgment. We call this "discretionary authority." We try to elect or appoint officials whose professional training and good character will lead them to apply rules with fairness, compassion, and fidelity to purpose. We may demand tighter rules and allow very limited discretion when officials can do great harm, as in the use of firearms by police. For the most part, however, we recognize that officials, to be responsible, must have some part in deciding what their duties require, including the possibility of ignoring or even violating an apparently binding rule.[2]

These observations show that responsibility rightly understood is not an enemy of moral freedom, if by that we mean making autonomous judgments in the light of principles, such as care for others or concern for the common good. Judgments based on reflection liberate people from the chains of conformity. But an ideal of moral responsibility remains, and this forecloses unfettered choice, or license to pursue short-term interests or self-destructive inclinations.[3]

THE CLAIMS OF IDENTITY

A good parent, teacher, citizen, or judge is likely to have a well-formed identity, including a clear idea of how he or she fits into a social world. Identity is an aspect of personality or, as we sometimes say, of selfhood. A person's identity emerges from the experience of being raised by particular parents; belonging to a particular family, religion, or social class; or from making life choices, such as marriage, a job, or a hobby. Most people have multiple identities: a woman can be wife, mother, teacher, lawyer, Methodist; a man can be husband, father, businessman, sailor. Identities are not necessarily permanent, and only some are really important or salient. Even salient identities are often resisted and transformed: people drift away from their families, change their names and religions. The more seriously people take their identities, the stronger are their feelings of responsibility, which may go well beyond external conformity.

Thus responsibility depends on how deeply we have internalized the values that govern the parts we play and the positions we hold. The more nuanced the understandings and judgments, the more does responsibility depend upon the formation of a distinctive

2. See Mortimer R. Kadish and Sanford H. Kadish, *Discretion to Disobey: A Study of Lawful Departures from Legal Rules* (Stanford, Calif.: Stanford University Press, 1973).

3. This is the implicit argument in Alan Wolfe's *Moral Freedom* (New York: W. W. Norton, 2001).

identity. Forming identities is a large part of specialized and professional training.[4]

Anchored Identities. The surest foundations of personal responsibility are bonds of kinship, nationality, locality, religion, race, and ethnicity. These we may call "anchored" identities, because they are based on feelings of rootedness and authenticity. Not everyone honors such obligations. Some people are more strongly influenced by cosmopolitan ideals or professional identities. However, most people take anchored identities seriously, feel comforted by them, and are moved by them to care for children, parents, and community members.

Anchored identity springs from very deep human needs for giving and receiving nurture, protection, and acknowledgment. These identities tell us most clearly who we are, rather than what we are as determined by tests and achievements. Our lives are bound up with those closest to us in kinship, friendship, or shared allegiance; who are most directly affected by what we do or neglect; who are vulnerable to us, and depend on us. Some such connections are transitory, leading to obligations but not sustained identities, as in the case of a driver involved in a car accident. Anchored identities are more lasting; the obligations they create are more indefinite or open-ended, and may be more demanding. The well-being of another person becomes a condition of one's own satisfaction and self-esteem. In this morality of the "significant other," we look to the flourishing of children, friends, and communities, rather than only to their injuries or urgent needs.

Expanded Identities. The reach of special obligations has no clear limits. Distant relations may be included, as well as close kin, friends, neighbors, co-religionists, fellow immigrants, fellow soldiers, fellow citizens. Thus, even "special" obligations may broaden or expand. Moreover, some anchored identities endure, while others are lost. In Western history, for example, many local and ethnic identities were eclipsed by the rise of the nation-state.

Expanded identities blur the line between personal and collective responsibility. As identities expand, so do the circles by which

---

4. Institutions as well as persons have distinctive identities. Among colleges, hospitals, foundations, churches, government agencies, and many business firms, strong identities produce clearer missions and more effective strategies. Institutional identities weaken when, for example, banking becomes like any other business, undisciplined by a special connection to financial safety and prudence.

we define who is kin and who is a stranger. Therefore the expansion of identities, as in the creation of a "European" identity, is a prime strategy for enhancing responsibility.

BROAD AND NARROW SELF-INTEREST

If responsibility is grounded in identity and selfhood, what shall we make of "self-interest" and "self-regard"? Does self-interest necessarily offend morality? One way of acting out of self-interest is to nurture or protect a distinctive identity. Being a good brother or a good judge raises questions of honor, integrity, authenticity, and self-esteem. Here self-interest is tied to the values we make our own, the standards we try to meet, the purposes we set for ourselves. The big question is, am I being true to the kind of person I want to be? This is an expression of broad or "systemic" self-interest, which puts in play one's whole personality, or salient features of it.

The alternative is self-interest more narrowly understood, driven by the quest for immediate gratifications or short-term advantages. Some particular benefit, such as a sexual encounter, an increment of prestige, a better-paying job, a profit margin, a television rating, or an election victory becomes the sole criterion of success. Scant attention is given to other values and other interests, including integrity and character.

The difference between broad and narrow self-interest was appreciated by Alexis de Tocqueville, who observed that the Americans of his time put great store by "self-interest rightly understood,"[5] sustained by such traits of character as self-discipline and trustworthiness. These "bourgeois" virtues encourage hard work, thrift, and investment, and rest on shared understandings of what it means to be a respectable merchant, farmer, or banker; they demand self-scrutiny, including the ability to distinguish avarice from profit and greed from gain. They restrain raw or unmitigated self-seeking.

Broad self-interest is not necessarily high-minded or indifferent to advantage. It brings strategic thinking into play—for example, when a company decides that its interests are better served by collective

---

5. Alexis de Tocqueville, *Democracy in America* (1840; reprint, New York: Alfred A. Knopf, 1956), vol. 2, p. 121.

bargaining and labor-management cooperation than by a zero-sum conflict. "Self" and "interest" take on new meanings when attention shifts from tactics to strategy, from short-term to long-term outcomes. Strategic self-interest is often more uncertain than short-term gain, but it promises greater security and more abundant prosperity. The price is deferred gratification.

Narrow self-interest is not always bad or unjustified. On the contrary, it is often the motor that drives and the indulgence that sustains a flourishing group life. Practical, short-term incentives are needed if people are to do the hard work required to nurture a marriage, a friendship, a church, or a political organization. Ideals and long-run objectives may have great appeal, but by themselves they may not be able to mobilize energies or induce sacrifice. They must be reinforced by practical benefits, realized sooner rather than later. This principle is well understood by organizers of all kinds, military as well as civilian, by pastors as well as politicians, educators as well as businessmen. The challenge is to transform narrow into broad self-interest, in part by teaching virtue, in part by offering appropriate incentives. With proper design, government, education, and industry can encourage initiative, release energies, enhance cooperation, and fix accountability. Virtue is taught, not only by rewarding good conduct and punishing misbehavior, but also by helping people feel good about themselves.

ON BEING PRINCIPLED

Broad self-interest—self-interest "rightly understood"—is closely connected to self-esteem, and self-esteem is furthered when we are guided by principle rather than expediency. To be principled is to uphold ideals in the course of complex decision-making—that is, while respecting other interests and other values. People who are principled, we say, are morally reliable. Committed to ideals, they convincingly exhibit moral coherence. Unswayed by vagrant pressures and short-term satisfactions, they "believe in something," they have integrity.

Being principled should not be confused with being dogmatic or governed by a hardened ideology. Ideologues paint simplified pictures of the social world, and they think those pictures give them sure guides to policy. Ideological thinking is a parody of principle, not the expression of subtle and demanding ideals.

There is nothing inherently wrong with abstract ideas. All thought is in some degree abstract; every classification, indeed every idea, is an abridgment of reality. Abstractions are dangerous when they rely for persuasion on unexamined preconceptions and on the power of suggestion, instead of on careful thought and reliable evidence.

The abiding sin of undisciplined abstraction is the temptation to overreach, usually by claiming too much for an idea or principle while willfully or unconsciously overlooking important differences and necessary qualifications. This temptation afflicts all argument, if only for reasons of clarity and style, but it is especially prevalent and pernicious when arguments are driven by political or polemical passion.

We cannot be principled without piercing the veil of rhetoric, without remaining faithful to context, without appreciating the interdependence of means and ends. We may want to treat our children equally, but we have to be realistic about how they differ in needs and talents, and how those differences justify our treating them differently or the same. We may endorse principles of limited government, environmental protection, a safety net for the poor, or international cooperation, but in doing so we cannot be indifferent to tradeoffs required among these and other values. We cannot be both principled and rigorously single-minded. Indeed, it is irresponsible to allow a single objective or a single precept to govern all decisions. Therefore principled decision is no stranger to compromise, nor is it a justification for ignoring or slighting other legitimate concerns. Being principled is not an easy road to virtue.

This point of view was expressed, in much the same spirit, by the great German sociologist Max Weber. In a famous lecture he dwelt on the difference between an "ethic of responsibility" and an "ethic of conviction" based on moral absolutes.[6] He cited as examples of moral absolutism the Mosaic code and the Sermon on the Mount. An ethic of moral absolutes says, "Follow the precept, whatever the consequences; let justice prevail, though the heavens fall." In contrast, Weber argued that public life requires an ethic of responsibility. We cannot govern by following an unqualified precept, such as "resist not evil," because statesmen must consider the effects of what

---

6. Max Weber, "Politics as a Vocation," in H. H. Gerth and C. Wright Mills, *From Max Weber: Essays in Sociology* (New York: Oxford University Press, 1946), pp. 77–128.

they and others do on the welfare of the political community as a living entity, a going concern. This means taking account of multiple interests, competing values, and changing circumstances. With these difficulties in mind, Weber said of politics that it is a "slow boring of hard boards."

Yet Weber could not wholly reject the "ethic of conviction" and the authority of moral absolutes. Although he began his discussion by asserting that the two moralities are very different and even incompatible, he concluded with a plea for reconciliation:

> It is immensely moving when a *mature* man—no matter whether
> young or old in years—is aware of a responsibility for the conse-
> quences of his conduct and really feels such responsibility with heart
> and soul. He then acts by following an ethic of responsibility and
> somewhere he reaches the point where he says: "Here I stand; I can
> do no other." . . . And every one of us who is not spiritually dead must
> realize the possibility of finding himself at some time in that position.
> Insofar as this is true, an ethic of ultimate ends and an ethic of respon-
> sibility are not absolute contrasts but rather supplements.[7]

In this passage we see Weber struggling to reconcile two conceptions of moral responsibility. Moral philosophers would say that the ethic of responsibility is "consequentialist." But consequences for what? This is a question too often unanswered. For Weber, an ethic of responsibility centers on the survival and welfare of a political community. However, an ethic of conviction (or of "ultimate ends") is no less concerned with consequences. It responds to the question, consequences for what? by asking, how will what I do affect my (or our) character, identity, and self-respect? An ethic of conviction makes selfhood the main concern. At some point, says Weber, a political leader must be prepared to say, "Here my fundamental values are at stake; here my integrity must be defended. I must be prepared to leave office and accept defeat rather than lose my integrity and betray my ideals."

The reconciliation Weber has in mind speaks to a basic ambivalence in moral experience. Morality is other-regarding, but is importantly self-regarding too. In Weber's ethic of conviction, we are

7. Ibid., p. 127.

responsible for what we are and have done, and to the ideal self we seek to form and strengthen. Here concern for consequences has a reflexive or internal relevance, and is in that sense self-regarding. Each kind of responsibility takes consequences seriously. One looks to the practical needs of a community or institution, the other to personal and institutional integrity. This analysis suggests that responsibility has two dimensions, which coexist, compete, and reinforce one another. Neither would determine policy by consulting raw self-interest or simple expediency.

These different ways of being responsible shed light on the moral dilemmas experienced by many during the 1840s and 1850s, before the onset of the American Civil War. The antislavery abolitionists followed an ethic of conviction: abolish slavery completely, immediately, even if this requires a breakup of the Union. Others rejected this moral purity and, like Abraham Lincoln, desired to save the Union. Although Lincoln's stand may properly be considered an ethic of responsibility, it shows that such an ethic is not divorced from idealism. What occurred was a clash of principles, not a sharp divergence between principle and opportunism.[8]

Compromise. We cannot judge the integrity of a policy by looking at externals alone, such as whether a compromise has been reached, including one that calls for "splitting the difference." Splitting the difference is often scorned as immoral or opportunistic, but it is defensible when the disputants must live together and cooperate, or when their claims have roughly equal intrinsic merit. Balancing values and accommodating interests can be an exercise of responsible leadership (and justified expedience) if core values are protected, perhaps by a creative policy or strategy.[9]

A compromise is unprincipled—indeed, is no true compromise at all—if it is mainly rhetorical or cosmetic, without promise of a constructive outcome. And if reconciliation is a relevant principle, some kinds of compromise are inescapable and desirable. Everything

8. For a recent account of the abolition movement, see Henry Mayer, *All on Fire: William Lloyd Garrison and the Abolition of Slavery* (New York: St. Martin's Press, 1998).

9. For example, a religious studies program in a public college can meet a demand that religion be taken seriously in its curriculum while protecting the integrity of the college by confining the program to historical and comparative analysis, without advocating or favoring particular beliefs. Such a solution might be debatable, but it is not necessarily craven or opportunistic.

depends on the nature of the compromise and just how principles affect it. It is not compromise as such that should be rejected, but compromise divorced from the values that should govern its course and outcome.[10]

10. In a new preface to *TVA and the Grass Roots* (1949; reprint, New York: Harper Torchbooks, 1966), I wrote (p. xiii): "This was not a case of simple compromise made by an organization capable of retaining its internal unity. Rather, a split in the character of the agency was created. As a result the TVA was unable to retain control over the course of the basic compromise. Concessions were demanded and won which may not have been essential if there had been fundamental unity within the organization. If there is a practical lesson for leadership here, it is this: if you have to compromise, guard against organizational surrender."

CHAPTER 4

A UNITY OF UNITIES

As frameworks for the conduct of self-directed lives, communities have this remarkable feature: they build upon and are nourished by other unities, which are persons, groups, practices, and institutions. These components characteristically claim respect and protection; they demand and are granted a variable, contested, but irreducible autonomy. What we prize in community is not unity of any sort at any price, but unity that preserves the integrity of the parts.

This organic unity is very different from the disciplined subordination and conformity we find in administrative or military hierarchies. In those settings subordinate units are deployable and even expendable. They can be modified or rearranged at will in the light of top-down decisions regarding purposes and policies. The logic of community is very different. Insofar as a special-purpose enterprise or agency becomes a community, its components are less readily manipulated or cast away.

A persistent preoccupation with the integrity of the parts lends a special significance to the experience of community. To be sure, effective communities are in some sense well-integrated. But what kind of integration? That is the nub. In a unity of unities the coherence of the whole allows and fosters the survival and flourishing of its fundamental components.

THE FEDERAL PRINCIPLE

In 1788, writing No. 51 of *The Federalist,* James Madison rejoiced that it would be practical to advance the republican cause "by a judicious modification and mixture of the *federal principle.*"[1] What is this principle? Is its meaning exhausted by what it says about the structure of government, affecting national and local jurisdictions? Or should we find in it a more basic guide to freedom and order? Is it a principle of community as well as of government?

The federal principle has Hebraic and Christian roots. The word *federal* derives from the Latin *foedus,* "treaty." In biblical history the transactions of God and humanity take the form of covenants or treaties. A covenanted people accept subordination to God, but they do so as free persons entering into a sacred compact. This tradition can be understood as an assertion of human dignity. It is a way of saying that people-in-community are responsible actors, capable of holding their own even against God. They have an irreducible claim to respect and concern. It is this that justifies calling the subordination to God a "federal" union.

"Federal" theology was developed mainly by Protestant thinkers. Hence, the emphasis is on faith, commitment, and the ultimate autonomy of individual persons. The federal idea can also be understood as a principle of social order. Thus in the thought of Althusius (1557–1638) a society is the product of many interwoven social unions, all based on explicit or tacit agreements.

These are not the covenants (as in feudalism) where freedom is forgone in exchange for protection. Nor are they the social contract of later generations. Althusius's conception of a federated unity is more pluralist than individualist. He could not accept the view expressed by his younger contemporary, Thomas Hobbes, that autonomous groups are "lesser Common-wealths in the bowels of the greater, like wormes in the entrayles of a naturall man."[2]

A more congenial idea is the Catholic doctrine of subsidiarity. In what has come to be a canonical formulation Pope Pius XI said, "It is a grave evil and a disturbance of right order, to transfer to the larger and higher collectivity functions which can be performed and pro-

---

1. James Madison in *The Federalist* (1788; reprint, New York: Modern Library, 1937), No. 51, p. 341.
2. Hobbes, *Leviathan* (1651; reprint, London: Pelican Books, 1968), p. 375.

vided for by lesser and subordinate bodies."[3] This doctrine differs from the Protestant "federal" tradition in that consent and agreement are not taken to be foundations of social order. Rather, local groups and institutions make indispensable contributions to human life, especially the flourishing of individual persons. What matters is well-being, not agreement. The constituent units of society have intrinsic worth. As objects of moral concern, they should be nourished and protected, helped to grow in inner strength. And their well-being demands a measure of self-determination. Good parents follow a principle of subsidiarity when they help their children grow, always aware of the child's intrinsic worth and need for independence.[4]

Despite this difference covenantal federalism and subsidiarity come to much the same conclusion. Each sees major social groups as morally responsible, and as necessary components of society. This is another way of saying that community is a unity of unities. There is no question of a world without diversity and conflict. The common theme is pluralism, tempered by loyalties, cabined by interdependence.

INDIVIDUALS AS PERSONS

Within a unity of unities the most important unity is the individual person. We diminish the experience of community, or create fake communities, when we treat people as instruments or objects, without needs of their own. Military, industrial, or educational organizations become communities insofar as they exhibit concern for persons. Only if we take people seriously, for their own sakes, as distinct, integrated, multifaceted beings, can the promise of community be fulfilled.[5]

In ordinary English an "individual" is a single human being.

3. Pius XI, *Quadragesimo anno*, 1931.

4. Subsidiarity is not the same as administrative decentralization, which is compatible with the premise that the parts are expendable as well as subordinate.

5. In Immanuel Kant's famous dictum, "Act so that you treat humanity, whether in your own person or that of another, always as an end and never as a means only," note that Kant speaks of treating people as "means *only*." This does not preclude employment, military service, and other activities that use people as means to ends. The force of the dictum is that when we do so, we should also recognize the special status persons have. This recognition enjoins practical limits on how people are used and for what ends. The quotation is from Immanuel Kant, *Foundations of the Metaphysics of Morals*, trans. Lewis White Beck (1785; reprint, New York: Liberal Arts Press, 1959), p. 47.

There is no necessary connotation of religious, political, or economic "individualism"; no prejudgment about the extent to which people are self-reliant or dependent, autonomous or subordinate. This reminder is needed because, in the liberal doctrines of modernity, people are thought of as free and independent, makers of their own lives, authors of their own intentions, unencumbered by obligations they did not choose. In that tradition, group membership should be voluntary, and contract based on mutual consent is the best way of organizing social life.

This "individualist" doctrine has both darkened and brightened the prospects for humanity. Liberal ideas are attractive because they treat people as free and equal members of a political community, without regard for their special histories or connections. This doctrine underpins democracy and enriches the rule of law. Yet the image of a self-referring, self-determining, self-sufficient individual is morally shortsighted. Lost from view or dimly perceived are responsibility, caring, authenticity, and commitment.

The alternative is a communitarian conception of individuals as socially embedded persons, products of history and culture, neither idealized nor abstract. Each life is infused with obligation, and each is an object of caring and concern. There is nothing "individualistic" in thinking about people in this way. Individual persons are not necessarily detached or independent, and they may or may not be wholly free to make or remake their beliefs or connections. Nor is there anything "individualistic" in demanding basic liberties. However deeply implicated people may be in the lives of others or in the requirements of social life, their well-being requires protected zones of privacy and security.

Consider what it means to treat employees as persons. To do so requires caring for them as self-realizing unities, not as faceless units of labor or achievement. It means trying to meet their personal needs for respect, compassion, and growth. People do not thrive in isolation or in wholly impersonal settings. To be treated "as a person" is to be acknowledged as someone whose character is formed in the course of interaction with others, one who has coworkers and family to enjoy and worry about.

We do not say that the "abstract individual" is a wholly irrelevant or pernicious idea. Treating individuals as persons emphasizes love rather than justice. But, to continue the example, good employee relations must offer justice as well as love, and here the liberal imagination comes into its own. For the benefit of law, justice, and democracy, we cannot avoid "abstracting" people from their special connections and settings. We have to treat them as members of a category (employee, citizen, passenger) if rules are to be applied with fairness and equality. However, we depart from this abstraction in important ways. We return to the concrete when, in doing justice, we take account of individual circumstances, and when, in designing institutions, we keep in mind the welfare of individual children, students, employees, citizens.

Individual persons are created, sustained, and sometimes deformed by their social worlds. They need protections as well as opportunities. Isolation and alienation are sometimes beneficial, for some people, but mostly they are prescriptions for suffering and despair.

Communitarians do not accept the view that culture and social life are irredeemably oppressive and "hegemonic." Of course, culture may be transmitted in subtle and insidious ways; children grow into a world they take for granted, and that world may be deceptive, oppressive, or corrupt. Much else, however, is benign and indispensable. Without the ideals and disciplines we gain from social life, we cannot know what is worth having and doing. We cannot discern our own true interests and those of others.

Therefore, a balance must be struck between the demands of society and the needs of individuals. Striking this balance is greatly helped by person-centered institutions, especially families, churches, and schools. Many organizations try to be more person-centered by supporting day-care centers and morale-building activities, such as company picnics, worker-friendly communication, and opportunities to benefit from the success of the enterprise. In our time person-centeredness is at risk. Fear of this loss has been at the heart of dissatisfaction with modernity. This fear has sometimes led people to embrace regimes that offer a Faustian bargain: solidarity whose price is ecstatic subordination. This outcome is a parody of community, not a realization of it.

CIVIL SOCIETY

The communitarian conception of a "unity of unities" finds much resonance today in discussions of "civil society." The phrase has a long history, and its meaning has changed in important ways. A

constant theme, however, is the need for a strong social fabric unfettered by government. Civil society is the largely self-generating
and self-regulating world of private groups and institutions—family,
business, advocacy, sports, locality, religion, ethnicity. Here ordinary lives are lived, mostly unvexed by a distant and impersonal authority; here freedom, reciprocity, and mutual aid are nurtured. Civil
society is the preeminent realm within which energies are liberated
and well-being is enhanced. It is also a brake on government. Without a vibrant civil society, government is likely to be unrestrained
and unresponsive.

In Eastern Europe, as the hold of communism weakened, voices
were heard on behalf of civil society. The anticommunist struggle in
Poland began among shipyard workers, who formed a union-based
movement called Solidarity, and that effort was supported by an increasingly independent Roman Catholic Church. These fateful stir-
rings revealed the importance of autonomous institutions, outside
government and capable of mounting opposition to it. This experience reaffirmed a major theme in liberal political philosophy: that
pluralism must be a social reality as well as a governing doctrine.[6]

All societies are composed of different, often contending groups
based on kinship, age, occupation, and inequalities of property or
power. Pluralism finds in this natural diversity a benign disorder, a
vital source of energy and safety. Dispersed and countervailing power
will limit centralized government, train alternative leaders, create
strong and autonomous associations. The idea is to domesticate
government, not destroy it or try to do without it. Pluralism prizes
institutions of human scale, "close to the people," accessible, responsive to local needs. In a pluralist system, people belong to a larger
community, such as a nation, not only as individual citizens but also
as members of families, churches, professions, and other specialized
groups. These "intermediate associations" stand guard between
government and individuals. They are havens of protection from impersonal authority. For many, they are also ladders of opportunity to
recognition and success.

Looking Outward and Inward. The pluralist ideal seeks to strengthen
community, not weaken it. However, if pushed too far, society falls

---

6. The tension between pluralist ideals and the realities of Solidarity and the
Roman Catholic Church in Poland is analyzed by Martin Krygier in "The Sources
of Civil Society," *Quadrant* (Melbourne), October 1996.

apart. The danger is greatest when religious or ethnic solidarity leads to demands for "self-determination" in the form of political autonomy or independence. The question becomes, What should be the focus of loyalty, piety, and benevolence? Should we look *inward* to our special affiliations and obligations? Or should we look *outward* to a broader fellowship?

In the language of sociology and philosophy, the choice is between "particularist" and "universalist" sentiments. Particularism is an ethic of commitment to people and institutions we care about because they are related to us in some special way, usually based on kinship, religion, or a local way of life. A classic expression of particularism is nepotism—hiring or doing business with relatives (or fraternity brothers) in preference to outsiders. Universalism, by contrast, is an inclusive morality. A crucial step in that direction is the embrace of strangers as belonging to one's own kind and as members of one's own community. In a universalist ethic, special origins and connections are set aside. Instead, only objective or impersonal criteria are appropriate, such as age, sex, need, talent, achievement, or, perhaps, being "children of God." The classic expression of universalism is political and legal equality.

Each perspective stems from and speaks to a different aspect of social life. Each has natural foundations. The two principles coexist in every society, but particularism has a stronger foundation in human nature and has been more congenial to traditional society; therefore, it has dominated most of human experience. A universalist ethos is more congenial to modernity. It is rightly perceived and vigorously defended as the jewel in the crown of liberalism. Yet the two kinds of altruism are not wholly separate. They compete and interact. Thus, in the eighteenth and nineteenth centuries an ideal of national citizenship was much admired by liberal writers and statesmen, in part because national citizenship creates a loyalty that transcends parochial ties of locality, kinship, ethnicity, and religion. From the standpoint of liberal universalism, parochial bonds are obstacles to civic unity—remnants of an unenlightened past. Still, by the twentieth century many had learned that nationhood is a powerful particularity of its own. Today nationality is an obstacle to more comprehensive ideals—especially when nationality is based on ethnic identity.

Communitarians are not wedded to universalist ideals. They see much worth in particularism, especially the benefits that close attachment can bring to a secure sense of self. The virtues of loyalty, authenticity, and commitment flourish when people share a unique history and connect their lives to particular places, relationships, practices, and symbols. These benefits should be recognized and preserved, even at some cost to universalist ideals.

Civilizing Civil Society. Civil society and pluralism are prima facie goods, but we still have to evaluate and judge them. The word *civil* is a clue. What should we expect of "intermediate" institutions beyond their own survival and vitality, beyond being bulwarks against real or potential despotism? How shall we assess, and how shall we remedy, the deficiencies of civil society, as measured by criteria of the common good? If these questions deserve answer, we cannot treat civil society as whatever is left over when we go outside government, or even as whatever lies between the economy and the state. The components of civil society differ in many ways, especially in their potential for good or evil.

In commerce and industry we recognize uncivil potentials for arbitrary authority, human exploitation, consumer fraud, pollution, and egregious waste of natural resources. Here civilizing civil society requires much more than the limited "bourgeois" virtues of thrift and fair dealing. We ask business enterprises to meet higher standards of responsible conduct. Insofar as they are "private governments," we expect them to administer, or collaborate in constructing, systems of industrial justice. We expect them to take responsibility for the consequences of their actions, and especially to bear their fair share of the full costs of production and marketing.

The most important evils in civil society are bigotry and hatred spawned by religious and ethnic differences. Therefore, a prime objective is the containment of militant fundamentalism—that is, of uncompromising and aggressive claims to religious, ethnic, or ideological purity. A religious orthodoxy can be respected so long as it sets itself apart, asking only to be undisturbed, without asserting the right to impose its own vision if it wins power in the political community.

Claims to respect must be tested; toleration has limits. Every individual and every group must meet threshold standards of moral acceptability. We cannot overlook or excuse racism, ethnic cleansing, religious persecution, and genocide. To civilize these impulses is to moderate them. Moderation begins by denying that any group can claim moral perfection and privileged truth.

THE MULTICULTURAL TEMPTATION

Earlier I noted that communities exhibit an irrepressible tension between inclusion and exclusion, between looking inward and outward, between maintaining unity and recognizing a broad range of interests and identities. This tension finds expression in the mandate of the First Amendment that "Congress shall make no law respecting an establishment of religion, or prohibiting the free exercise thereof." In proposing this amendment, as part of the Bill of Rights, the first Congress sought to uphold ideals of toleration and mutual respect. It extended the boundaries of community by rejecting the idea that any particular "faith community" could say what those boundaries should be. The "free exercise" clause protects diversity in faith and conscience. As the nation came to include more Catholics, Jews, and nonbelievers, the line between church and state had to be redrawn, a process that has continued, and will continue, so long as religion is a significant part of American life.

Why Diversity? In the last decades of the twentieth century, the virtues of diversity were loudly proclaimed. There was, at the same time, an apparent waning of assimilation and integration as American ideals. American institutions, it was said, "should look like America."[7] A quest for recognition—as fully enfranchised parts of the nation—was high on the agenda of groups long marginalized and kept down. The trend was in part a quest for inclusion, in part a spillover into mainstream consciousness of relativist ideas hitherto confined to modernist intellectuals. These currents united to form what came to be known as multiculturalism, whose watchwords are difference and diversity. The aim is self-determination, *without giving up inclusion.*

As the constitutional protection of religious freedom shows, diversity of a sort has long been honored in the American political community. In addition, immigrants of all kinds long maintained a vibrant ethnic life, with their own newspapers, schools, and religious institutions. Toleration in America began as a policy of prudence; there was already substantial religious diversity at the time of the nation's founding. But something more than prudence was in play,

7. This was the way President Clinton introduced the members chosen for his cabinet in 1996.

something more subtle and more fundamental. This was the belief that free people, in the groups to which they belong, must be able to express their own conceptions of selfhood and identity. The clear cases are religion and kinship, which by extension include ethnic identity. In this way, an ideal of diversity unites freedom and rooted-ness; it vindicates the right to be connected, in some deep way, to what one takes to be the source of one's being.

Diversity is not self-justifying. It should be good for the community. Therefore, a claim to the recognition of difference is subject to scrutiny and may be rejected. We do not believe that Mafia "families," juvenile gangs, or extremist political or religious sects are examples of desirable diversity. A threshold standard of morality must be met.

Sovereignty and Self-determination. A culture is best preserved and developed when a people can have its own language, its own modes of thought, its own institutions—in short, when they are protected by a principle of self-determination, which enjoins respect for different ways of life, different expressions of the human spirit. Respect and self-determination belong together and reinforce one another. However, people who claim rights of self-determination must be ready to accord respect to others. They have no license to do as they please if that means disregarding the interests of others.

Among nations, self-determination means international recognition of territorial borders and unfettered control over internal affairs. This "sovereignty" has helped create more or less independent national economies and nationally defined systems of law and democracy. It is not likely that, in the foreseeable future, nations will forgo these and other benefits. Yet in the twentieth century many heinous crimes were committed under the color of sovereignty. The idea of sovereignty is tarnished and has lost much of its hold on the political, legal, and moral imagination.

Human rights have gained much support from changes in public opinion and from new international institutions. Limits have been placed on what nominally sovereign rulers can do to their own citizens and to others under their control. In the developing law of nations, sovereignty is no sure defense against charges of genocide, ethnic cleansing, or mass killings and deportations. Although national sovereignty is far from dead, it can be overridden by a showing of gross misconduct.

Hard and Soft Multiculturalism. "We are all multiculturalists now," writes a veteran analyst of race and ethnicity in America. What Nathan Glazer has in mind, however, is a very moderate version of that doctrine: "When I say multiculturalism has won, and that we are all multiculturalists now, I mean that we all now accept a greater degree of attention to minorities and women and their role in American history and social studies and literature classes in schools. . . . Multiculturalism is, in its own way, a universalistic demand: All groups should be recognized."[8] I call this soft multiculturalism because it is so undemanding and easy to accept. Guided by ideals of reconciliation and inclusion, soft multiculturalism turns away from schoolbooks that ignore the legacy of slavery in America; from public arts and ceremonies that present white Anglo-Saxon Protestant (WASP) America as the nation's preferred self-image; from a community ignorant of and inhospitable to the rich histories, sensibilities, and accents of nonwhite and hyphenated Americans.

This humane philosophy of inclusion and acceptance is by no means opposed to integration and assimilation. It speaks to the terms and strategies of such a policy. Like Glazer, communitarians reject *coercive* assimilation, which was practiced for too long in the treatment of Native Americans. Coercive assimilation seeks to extinguish special identities, even if doing so destroys families and makes children feel ashamed of their racial or ethnic origins. A better policy seeking integration of minorities will be governed by norms of respect and conservation.

Soft multiculturalism is not a fighting faith. For this reason it is unattractive among those whose main purpose is to expose and avenge an oppressive past. For them, soft multiculturalism is too tame. They would rather have a pluralism detached from any basic commitment to the larger unity it seeks to shape and perfect. This is the multicultural temptation, whose preferred strategy is confrontation, whose cost is fragmentation. Struggle not reconciliation, division not unity, drive the policies of hard multiculturalism.

The multicultural temptation has led to extravagant claims, such as the idea that assimilation is genocide if it results in the extinction

---

8. Nathan Glazer, *We Are All Multiculturalists Now* (Cambridge: Harvard University Press, 1997), pp. 13–14. Glazer focuses on education, but his reference is much wider.

of a distinctive culture or way of life.[9] However, genocide is a great crime, not because it destroys a culture, but because it kills people. To be sure, it is an offense to obliterate a culture with hostile intent. But cultures may fade and be replaced for many reasons, some very wrong, others more acceptable. True genocide is beyond excuse.

Hard multiculturalism makes an easy transition from the valid claim that folk medicine should be taken seriously to the unwarranted conclusion that all medicine is folk medicine or, more generally, that scientific method is a myth.

Cultural diversity is a good, but not an absolute or unquestionable good. The arbiter is our best understanding of what makes for a good human life. Therefore, no serious harm can be justified by an appeal to self-determination. We reject not only genocide but human sacrifice, torture, slavery, and much else that stems from ignorance, fear, and the abuse of power.

Communitarians are not radical relativists. They accept principles that transcend cultures and speak to our common humanity. Among these is the federal principle, which prizes diversity, and unity as well. This dual concern is at the heart of communitarian policy.

---

9. Coercive assimilation is sometimes very shocking, as in the Australian policy during the first half of the twentieth century of forcibly removing indigenous children from their families. This may account for some disposition to treat coercive assimilation as genocide. For reflections stimulated by the Australian experience, see Raimond Gaita, *A Common Humanity* (Melbourne: Text Publishing, 1999), pp. 107–130.

PART TWO

PROGRAMS

A STRONG SOCIAL FABRIC

RIGHTS IN THEIR PLACE

DEMOCRACY MADE GOOD

RESPONSIBLE ENTERPRISE

SOCIAL JUSTICE

CHAPTER 5

A STRONG SOCIAL FABRIC

The communitarian project begins with concern for the strength and resilience of social life. This is not a demand for strength or unity on any terms without counting costs in loss of freedom, stifled initiative, or stiff-necked resistance to change. What matters is the quality of life and the integrity of our institutions.

A FRAYING FABRIC

In the twentieth century economic, political, and cultural transformations have damaged the fabric of social life. These changes have included a great expansion of the number of women who work outside the home; uprooting and scattering of close relatives; more unstable jobs and careers; and acceptance of the separation of sex and marriage. These transformations have intensified earlier trends, especially industrialization and urbanization, which brought in their train the fateful divorce of household and work, education and family life. Some special features of American history—the experience and memory of a revolutionary struggle, the great westward migration, the spread of democracy, successive waves of immigration—made for an unruly culture, individualist, pluralist, careless of tradition, unburdened by a feudal past.

It is an irony of American history that the bonds of community have been loosened even as we have created a more homogeneous and more integrated national society. The same trends have resulted in the decline of kinship as a reliable resource for apprenticeship and opportunity. Moreover, the *detached* nuclear family has become the representative form of family life. The weakening of family ties has placed a great many children at risk.

Each of these trends has brought substantial benefits: economic prosperity, personal freedom, religious and ethnic diversity, a spirit of toleration. All this explains, and to some extent may excuse—but does not change—the underlying condition: a frayed social fabric in need of repair.

We should not try to reverse what is and should be irreversible, such as the waning of prejudice against women in employment and in the professions. Instead, we should seek new ways of enhancing personal and social responsibility. And we should address those corrosive ideas that have entered, almost imperceptibly, the assumptions and thoughtways of everyday life. Most important, for communitarians, is the emergence of what we may call a culture of limited commitment. As I suggested in chapter 2, this runs counter to the communitarian principle of open-ended obligation, which calls for commitment to others, including the groups and institutions to which we belong, as whole persons, in a spirit of loyalty, caring, and sacrifice. In all our important connections, much may be demanded of us that was unplanned and unexpected. Yet modern life, where so much is fluid and changing, makes lasting commitments hard to sustain, and many are reluctant to create them. Even more perilous is the taken-for-granted belief that limited commitment is a proper guide to what we should want and how we should live, in all spheres of life.

The principle of limited commitment shows up in many ways: marriages postponed or replaced by domestic partnerships; divorce as an easy option; neighbors who do not need each other; support groups encouraging openness but wanting in mutual commitment and interdependence; public opinion vulnerable to sound-bites and celebrity; pressures for short-term gains in corporate America. All are examples of cramped perspectives and loose ties. Their effects are uneven, of course, as is their significance for ordinary life. Taken together with more fundamental trends, such as those I have mentioned, and some I have not mentioned, they amply justify the wake-up message communitarians are sending to their fellow Americans.

We need not say that modern society is in a state of radical disarray. Rather, it is the direction that should concern us. To care about a child's character and moral development, we need not find full-blown alienation or delinquency. Character is or should be a constant preoccupation of parenting, and also of leadership. It helps to have vulnerabilities and dangers in mind, as when we recognize the power of peer groups in the lives of adolescents. For the United States, and for other Western countries, the danger is that we will drift into an epoch of disorder and impotence, and that we will do so without facing up to the challenges of modernity. Two centuries of sociological learning have taught us, in many ways, the negative impact of modernity on social bonds. In premodern times, and well into the present era, a person's identity was fixed by locality, religion, kinship, and occupation. These parameters brought stability and coherence to everyday life, but the costs were too high. In response, modernity created new unities to replace the old. In the process the world became more impersonal and more fragile. Wrong as they were in so many ways, Marx and Engels were close to the mark when they said, in *The Communist Manifesto* (1848), "All that is solid melts into air."

To deal with the problems of modernity, we must recognize its effect on community: thinned culture, rootlessness, an ethos of limited commitment. This does not lead us to reject modernity, or give up the great benefits it has brought. Rather, we must recognize that the benefits are not cost-free. The most important cost is a weakening of the social bonds on which we rely for mutual trust, cooperation, and commitment. These goods flourish when the social fabric is strong. They are endangered or lost when people are isolated and self-centered.[1]

---

1. The social fabric includes beliefs as well as connections: shared understandings about what is good to have and right to do, such as fulfilling obligations, taking pride in one's work, making sacrifices for others or for a cause. In sociological language, beliefs are part of culture, which brings coherence and texture to social life. Equally important are the practical, need-centered, life-enhancing connections that people have: a functional family, supportive friends and colleagues, associations of all kinds. These connections (which in sociology are called "social organization") create powerful incentives for holding to beliefs and transmitting them to the young. Mostly, the two realms reinforce one another. They sometimes conflict, as when the pull of belief breaks friendships or family ties.

LIBERAL MYOPIA

An ethos of limited commitment finds much comfort in liberal conceptions of individual freedom and public morality. Therefore we should look closely at an influential doctrine forcefully expressed by John Stuart Mill, writing in 1859:

> The object of this essay is to assert one very simple principle, as entitled to govern absolutely the dealings of society with the individual in the way of compulsion and control, whether the means used be physical force in the form of legal penalties, or the moral coercion of public opinion. That principle is, that the sole end for which mankind are warranted, individually or collectively, in interfering with the liberty of action of any of their number, is self-protection. That the only purpose for which power can be rightfully exercised over any member of a civilized community, against his will, is to prevent harm to others. His own good, either physical or moral, is not a sufficient warrant. . . . The only part of the conduct of anyone, for which he is amenable to society, is that which concerns others. In the part which merely concerns himself, his independence is, of right, absolute. Over himself, over his own body and mind, the individual is sovereign.[2]

A "very simple principle"? Not really. A ringing affirmation of liberty? Certainly. Mill was asserting the freedom to decide for oneself what to think and how to live. In our basically liberal society this principle has great appeal. Nevertheless, much remains ambiguous. Mill's famous doctrine claims too much. Expressing as it does an ethos of individualism, it cannot be a reliable guide to social policy.

The most important ambiguity is the meaning of "harm to others." For Mill what counts as harm is injury to *individuals*. What concerns others is only their individual safety, property, liberties, and entitlements. The importance of a supportive and life-enhancing *environment* is slighted. Yet people have good reason to care about how the behavior of others affects the quality of their lives, which in turn depends on good social and moral environments. Therefore, people expect more than freedom from injury. They need a world made

---

2. J. S. Mill, *On Liberty* (1859), in *Utilitarianism, On Liberty, Considerations on Representative Government* (reprint, London: J. D. Dent, 1984), pp. 72–73.

liveable by decorum and self-restraint. Furthermore, injury may affect groups as well as individuals, and may be long-term as well as immediate.

The harm done to a moral environment is sometimes very clear, as when disruptions in a classroom degrade an environment of learning, or when the free expression of racist or sexist attitudes creates a "hostile work environment." Many environments need special protection; for example, the moral environment of family life is protected by the efforts parents make to be models for their children.

These concerns are far from trivial. They recognize harms that might come to a moral environment from gambling, drug abuse, pornography, public nudity, or prostitution. Such offenses have been called "crimes without victims" because the victim is often the very person who commits the offense, or someone willing to cooperate in it, such as a prostitute. In truth, the alleged harm is often difficult to define and may be highly controversial or only distantly related to the offending act. These are important cautions, but they do not do away with the need for public education and social control.

If a liberty is limited, it should be for good reason. Mill was right to say that some sort of harm must be done or threatened. But liberal myopia sees only what is near at hand. It will not do when we have to take account of subtle dangers and long-term effects, such as the consequences for culture and everyday life when drunkenness or drug abuse are rampant, when anyone can have a gun without restrictions, when traffic signals are routinely ignored—in short, when liberty becomes license. A community may properly be concerned about injury to the moral order, without apology and without waiting for total collapse or disintegration.[3]

It is surely wrong to suppose that every offense against conventional morality may be suppressed as a threat to the moral order. That leaves no room for openness and change, such as the changes we have

3. In a number of his writings the liberal theorist Ronald Dworkin has defended the importance of a "moral environment." In *Life's Dominion* (New York: Knopf, 1993), for example, he says that a woman's abortion decision should respect the sanctity of human life, thereby upholding a moral environment within which responsible choices can be made. "Society has a right, if its members so choose, to protect its culture from that kind of indifference, so long as the means it chooses do not infringe the rights of pregnant women to a choice" (p. 170). This is a step in a communitarian direction.

seen in sexual morality, including the growing acceptance of homosexuality. There is no escape from making judgments about what can be accepted and what is intolerable. Those judgments count the costs of limiting liberty, both in human suffering, as in the case of abortion or homosexuality, and in fostering criminality, as in America's failed effort to prohibit the production and sale of alcoholic beverages.

The most important question is when and how much to rely on criminal punishment. Criminal law is a very crude instrument, whose procedures and penalties are often destructive and dehumanizing. Homes are broken into, wrists are handcuffed, ankles are chained, people suffer the hardships of detention. Therefore, the criminalization of deviance should be avoided, especially the so-called "crimes without victims." Much can be made illegal or socially disapproved of, without being criminalized. Alternative remedies include education, as well as incentives and disincentives. Liberals tend to fudge this difference, as Mill did in formulating his "simple principle." If we decide that criminalization is ineffective, we may nevertheless believe that a practice such as drug addiction is harmful and should be discouraged and reduced as much as possible. We do not criminalize teen-age pregnancy, but we think that young women should have babies later and under better conditions. We can use public funds to support programs for education, rehabilitation, and whatever alternatives to criminalization may work. These alternatives are coercive in some ways; they require collective judgment and public money. Moreover, we cannot foreclose the possibility of using the criminal law when other sanctions are ineffective or unavailable.

Mill's principle is too broad because it extends to all forms of social control, not just to the harsh workings of criminal law. In the passage quoted above, Mill rejects coercion by "public opinion" as well as by "legal" penalties. This is an excessive limitation on what people can do collectively to protect the integrity of institutions or the quality of everyday life. Mill's policy would preclude a wide range of efforts to encourage better conduct in education, the professions, industry, the media, family life, and public spaces. In these settings the great task is to find a proper mix of instruction, incentive, and control. Coercion may consist only of taxes imposed for the support of public institutions, such as education or the arts. Mill's principle withdraws these concerns from effective public scrutiny and control. Liberty itself would be at risk, for it requires public nurture and support. We cannot defend a culture of liberty without asking what it requires to survive and flourish.

Liberal myopia may be traced to an excess of individualism. As Charles Taylor points out:

> Common purposes are only sustained to the extent that people do not identify themselves exclusively as individuals but also see themselves at least in part as essentially defined by their adherence to the political community. . . . But what it [liberalism] exalts as valuable is exclusively individual self-fulfillment, plus relations of fairness between these self-directing individuals. It offers a picture of human life in which common purposes have no valid place, in which they appear more often as potential obstacles to individual self-development.[4]

The alternative Taylor offers is "civic freedom," which transcends radical individualism and which nurtures the institutions and the shared understandings without which freedom is damaged, distorted, or lost. Without authority, without appropriate rules, individual freedoms cannot be protected. This truth is obscured when liberty is identified with self-expression and individuality.

BASELINE MORALITIES

In the interests of liberty people should endure some disorder, perhaps even some danger and abuse. We do not want a sanitized world of restraint and conformity. The spirit of youth should not be crushed. In a free society, dissent and provocation are expected and sometimes welcomed. Hence we must closely examine what we mean by "order" and what *kind* of order is appropriate in a city street, at a ball game, or at a church, school, or hospital.

A minimal or baseline morality is easily understood and readily accepted when safety and property are at risk. Every society punishes core crimes—notably murder, assault, robbery, burglary. Everyone agrees that in these cases society may restrict the liberty of offenders.

---

4. Charles Taylor, "Religion in a Free Society," in *Articles of Faith, Articles of Peace: The Religious Liberty Clauses and the American Public Philosophy*, edited by James Davison Hunter and Os Guinness (Washington, D.C.: Brookings Institution, 1990), pp. 109–110.

But what about the moral environment? Is this included among the harms Mill thought were the "sole evil" whose containment justifies social coercion? The true answer must be yes.

Consider the "broken windows" doctrine in community policing.[5] This is the idea that environments are degraded, and may be further degraded, if a pattern of minor offenses is ignored. A building or neighborhood with broken windows invites further breakage and more disrespect for the neighborhood. If nothing is done to halt the degradation, more serious harm can be expected. The social fabric of a community is endangered if the conditions of everyday life are considered unimportant, or left to take care of themselves.[6]

To protect the quality of life, we limit the location of certain businesses, such as slaughterhouses, gambling places, and sex shops. We have laws against public solicitation for prostitution, aggressive panhandling, and public nudity and copulation. These policies have well-known risks, including abuse of power by police and other officials. Legal controls are suspect insofar as they try to enforce a moral code without any finding of social harm and without taking account of significant changes in belief and practice. When enforcement relies on hard-to-define terms, such as "loitering" and "indecency," police and prosecutors have too much discretion, and this often leads to unfair treatment of stigmatized groups. These dangers call for patient scrutiny, better rules, and sophisticated judgment, not for indifference to the quality of life.

Communitarians do not shrink from coercion when it is justified by necessity and governed by respect for individual rights, the integrity of institutions, and the rule of law. But coercion is often ineffective and counterproductive. Furthermore, it runs counter to communitarian ideals of reconciliation, communication, and solidarity. If students at a high school routinely drop trash on school grounds,

5. George L. Kelling and Catherine Coles, *Fixing Broken Windows* (New York: Simon and Schuster, 1996).

6. A causal link between degraded environments and serious crimes may be questioned, as it is by Bernard E. Harcourt in *Illusion of Order* (Cambridge, Mass.: Harvard University Press, 2001), chap. 3. However, "disorder demoralizes communities, undermines commerce, leads to the abandonment of public spaces, and undermines public confidence in the ability of government to solve problems; fear drives citizens further from each other and paralyzes their normal order-sustaining responses, compounding the impact of disorder." See Kelling and Coles, *Fixing Broken Windows*, p. 242. Thus understood, protecting a moral envirnoment requires the cooperation of many institutions, not just law enforcement.

principals and their aides may promulgate rules and try to enforce them. Their main task, however, is to change the student culture, and the preferred means for doing so are communication and leadership. Such a strategy requires authority, but does not depend on coercion. We do not need more turmoil and more reasons for expelling students. Instead, we need more ways of encouraging self-respect, created by acts of personal and social responsibility. A social fabric is not mainly held together by coercion and domination. Although "law and order" strategies are sometimes justified, they are a sign of weakness and perhaps of desperation.

REPAIRING THE FABRIC

Communitarians argue that the social fabric must be protected and nurtured, even when we recognize the need for reform. Facing up to modernity requires change, but the changes should be sensitive to our continuing need for effective institutions and social coherence. There is no turning back; nostalgia will not do.

Social Capital as Moral Capital. The concept of "social capital" helps us understand what is at stake and what must be done. Social capital is formed when group life creates resources that help people work together and trust one another. People who associate with others effectively, and are guided by shared understandings and accepted rules, will more readily help one another, and show self-restraint. Intact families encourage children to study and parents to stick to their jobs. In industry, good personal relations among employees benefit morale, limit absenteeism, and reduce the cost of training new workers. Much of sociology is devoted to studying the varieties of social capital, their worth, and their costs.[7]

Modern institutions have depleted traditional forms of social capital, which are replaced by new forms based on new principles. A world largely devoted to agriculture, crafts, and small-scale trading drew heavily on bonds of kinship, and on occupational, religious, and political traditions. The new age of commerce brought fresh

7. On the theory of social capital, see James S. Coleman, *Foundations of Social Theory* (Cambridge, Mass.: Harvard University Press, 1990). Policy applications are explored in Robert D. Putnam, *Bowling Alone: The Collapse and Revival of American Community* (New York: Simon and Schuster, 2000).

sources of energy, new ways of organizing labor and aggregating investments. These transformations were uneven and incomplete, and for a long time the older forms of social capital remained important. The new capitalists relied on families to keep people at work, and they welcomed a labor force made docile by a heritage of deference and subordination.

In the nineteenth and twentieth centuries these social supports became less reliable. Families lost coherence when they were no longer economic units, no longer family farms or other businesses requiring authority, cooperation, and discipline; when they were pulled apart by the conflicting demands of work, schooling, and recreation; when two earners were needed to sustain an acceptable standard of living. Religion lost influence when it became "disestablished" in the hearts of the people as well as in the constitutional doctrine of the liberal state. The authority of government suffered as the demand for services, and for wise judgment, outran its competence. In most spheres of modern life we have seen a steady depletion of social capital, which is moral capital insofar as it sustains trust, responsibility, and cooperation.

From Tradition to Design.   To strengthen the social fabric and meet the challenges of modernity, we should look to innovation and the future as well as to tradition and the past. To remedy the depletion of social and moral capital, it may be wiser to rely on institutional design than on taken-for-granted practices and received thoughtways. Today's necessities demand even more resources than the past could offer, especially to provide jobs for new generations and care for elderly parents. The privileges and comforts of kinship were supported by traditional conceptions of morality, and by the rural and small-town settings of most people's lives. They were always supplemented, to some extent, by religious and philanthropic institutions. Today there is a much greater need for active engagement by the community as a whole, in caring for children, the elderly, and those who are handicapped, homeless, or unwanted.

However, it is a mistake to counterpose tradition and design. Instead, the design of caring institutions should be based on the funded experience of living communities. The designs should reflect and preserve what was positive and healthy in traditional ideas and practices. The extended family may contract and even wither, but the indispensable work of supplementing the nuclear family's obligation to provide secure, growth-enhancing environments for its members must go on. This requires public support of child care and early schooling, as well as family-friendly employment policies.

In *The Death and Life of Great American Cities*, Jane Jacobs shows how modern urban design can be guided by principles drawn from more organic forms of city life. She points to the importance of street-level diversity and of urban settings that encourage interaction, rather than isolation, resulting in more social control, including observation and supervision of street activities. Her book is a compelling reminder of what can be learned from a close study of traditional practices. She shows how we can glean useful lessons from the chaff of history.[8]

The Independent Sector. One source of social capital deserves special mention. This is the variously named "independent," "voluntary," "third," or "nonprofit" sector of society, composed of numerous organizations devoted to public and philanthropic purposes. These include private schools and colleges, foundations, research universities, advocacy groups, social service agencies, and many others. They are active at all levels, from international to local, pursuing many different interests.

Some components of the independent sector are subsidized by churches or foundations, while others depend on donations from individuals. Some run on the earnings they generate, and hence are best understood as limited-profit rather than nonprofit enterprises. Some have professional staffs, while others rely wholly on volunteers or on quasi-volunteers willing to work for low pay. Most are initiated and sustained by autonomous, self-generated groups or benefactors, and in that sense are "voluntary" associations. Most are largely independent of government, and of market pressures. Although many partnerships are formed with government or business, the initiative is usually theirs, as is the special energy and dedication they bring. They often reach beyond what government can or will do at a given time, and they are not limited by stringent criteria of investment and profit.

A vibrant independent sector seems wholly compatible with modern life. Its many and diverse components have flourished despite the predominance of business and the great expansion of government. Some have been created to counter business practices, such as

8. Jane Jacobs, *The Death and Life of Great American Cities* (New York: Random House, 1961).

oppressive working conditions and pollution, or as vehicles for criticism of government programs. The independent sector is in some ways a creature of government (benefiting from favorable tax policies), and it often depends on business for cooperation and support. Nevertheless, independence remains, and the independent sector can do much to make up for the failures of private and public bureaucracy.[9]

THE ROLE OF GOVERNMENT

I have been saying that under modern conditions the social fabric needs all the help it can get, including support from the organized political community—that is, from government. Communitarians believe in the moral primacy of the community over the state. Nevertheless, government is not necessarily alien, apart, or oppressive. It can and should be an integral part of society, a source of initiative and leadership for the common good. Government can enhance and invigorate social life. However, we have reason to worry about depending too much on government insofar as this results in a loss of self-discipline and self-reliance, when what we can and should do for ourselves is done by distant and impersonal agencies. We oppose welfare without work, for those who can work, and we want to be sure that the largely self-generating and self-regulating groups in society have genuine responsibilities and adequate resources. We do not want to empower government at the expense of grass-roots solidarity, engagement, and competence.

Another concern is that government is largely staffed by self-serving human beings and is often captured by special interests. Well-intentioned programs are often administered by officials who care little for interests not their own and who are less than faithful to public purposes and democratic principles.

These concerns are far from trivial. They are sufficiently well founded to justify rejection of an all-powerful state. However, they do not justify an automatic, unreflective distrust of government or a want of confidence that bureaucratic excesses can be controlled.

---

9. For background and comparative analysis, see Robert Wuthnow, ed., *Between States and Markets: The Voluntary Sector in Comparative Perspective* (Princeton, N.J.: Princeton University Press, 1991).

Communitarians do not counterpose state and society. This is another departure from liberal orthodoxy, which has made much of that opposition. For communitarians the collaboration of law, government, and society is a desirable and practical ideal. In its best forms, law and government are supported and enriched by social order and economic prosperity. When government and society are in harmony, people offer loyalty and obedience. They willingly pay taxes in support of a wide range of public purposes. For its part, government in a free society protects rights, acts in the light of legal principles, justifies those acts before impartial tribunals, and relies on the cooperation of private groups and institutions. The larger outcome is a system we call the rule of law.

The integration of law, government, and society calls for responsive institutions. A government is responsive when it protects its own integrity, mainly by adhering to constitutional principles, while remaining open to the claims of new interests and responsibilities, including interests hitherto unheard and responsibilites hitherto unmet. A responsive government views itself as part of a wider system of ideas and institutions, from which it draws its strength—and which demands participation.[10]

Consider the reinvention of community policing. This strategy is in part a reaction against "police professionalism," which had the effect of withdrawing police from community life by isolating them in patrol cars and limiting their responsibilities to fighting crime by answering emergency calls. The separation of police and community created a distant, impersonal force, out of touch with everyday events and ordinary conditions in neighborhoods and on the streets. Community policing widens responsibilities and enlarges police discretion. This has its dangers, but the strategy makes the police more accountable and accessible. Community policing builds bridges between law enforcement and the community. It cannot be successful without significant changes in leadership, organization, and policy.

Much experience has shown that private energies cannot be relied on, by themselves, to deal with pervasive poverty, injustice, and unregulated self-interest. We need public programs for retirement, medical care, environmental protection, education, public safety,

---

10. I return to the topic of responsive government below, p. 89.

national defense, international obligations, and much else that requires collective will, commitment, and sacrifice.

Government can help mobilize private energies for philanthropy and community service. These activities depend on leadership and organization, including effective recruitment, training, and supervision of volunteers. Volunteering is a great idea, but successful programs using volunteers are well funded and are led by professional staffs. Some resources come from private institutions, such as churches and foundations. The efforts of churches, however, often depend on unusually well-motivated individuals, and many foundations are interested in providing only seed money rather than continuing support. A sustained and comprehensive effort must look to the whole community, including all levels of government.[11]

THE ECOLOGICAL IMAGINATION

In thinking about the social fabric, we return again and again to the idea that society is not made up of free-standing or self-sufficient components. Every group, every individual needs freedom to develop distinctive abilities and identities. Left to themselves, however, they become insular, intrusive, or crowded out. Therefore, we cannot be comfortable with the separation of spheres. We look instead for bonds of interdependence and opportunities for cooperation. We bring to bear an ecological sensibility.

There is indeed a close connection between communitarian and ecological principles. The latter encourage appreciation for diverse populations and shared habitats; for the mutual adaptation of all elements, organic and inorganic; for the fragility of ecosystems. Both resist the exploitation of resources by heedless humans pursuing short-term satisfactions.

Most revealing, perhaps, is the communitarian and ecological commitment to what I referred to earlier as "a unity of unities." The

---

11. An example is the work of the Extension Service, coordinated by the Office of Cooperative Extension of the U.S. Department of Agriculture. Over many years this program helped farmers and farm families to be more efficient producers and live better lives by combining the resources of federal, state, and county governments, together with those of land-grant colleges. Many of the "county agents" provided leadership for local community organizations.

well-being of ecosystems depends on regard for the integrity of all components, on balanced diversity, not domination by a single species, such as a genetically uniform stand of corn or wheat. The motto is "handle with care." After human intervention, an ecosystem is healed by creating a new balance or restoring an old one.

In human communities, ecological awareness calls for prudent use of social capital: finding life-enhancing ways of overcoming destructive divisions, living within and protecting a distinctive habitat or environment. Ecological principles do not preclude conscious intervention. On the contrary, they support sensible planning for sustainable levels of use or production; they are necessary guides to rational intervention. The ecological imagination is a voice of resistance to policies that are careless of the quality of life, indifferent to supportive environments, unmoved by the need for a wider understanding of our interdependent lives.

CHAPTER 6

RIGHTS IN THEIR PLACE

The new communitarians have argued for the coupling of rights and responsibilities. Indeed, as I noted earlier, "Rights and Responsibilities" is the motto of their journal, *The Responsive Community*. Much has been written about the ways in which "rights talk" undermines sound public policy.[1] In this chapter we consider what this view of rights entails. We distinguish an appropriate assertion of rights from undisciplined rights-centeredness.

RIGHTS AND RIGHTS-CENTEREDNESS

Rights are the freedoms, powers, or benefits claimed by individuals or groups as morally justified or legally recognized or both. Rights come in many varieties. Some are well established, supported by broad consensus and a shared history; others, such as the rights created by ordinary contracts, are readily changed or extinguished. Some rights, such as freedom of speech or worship, are shored up by political passion, religious fervor, or a strong sense of justice.

Rights are often contested. In U.S. constitutional law, "due

---

1. See Mary Ann Glendon, *Rights Talk: The Impoverishment of Political Discourse* (New York: Free Press, 1991).

process" and "equality" have had uncertain and changing meanings, and this ambiguity has made steady work for lawyers, judges, philosophers, and historians. Arguments for moral or "natural" rights invoke theories of human nature and the human condition, while legal rights appeal to the authority of constitutions, statutes, customs, and judicial opinions. Moral and legal rights overlap and interact in complex ways. The difference is crucial for some purposes, such as knowing what obligations will be enforced by the courts. Also, we want to know what lies behind the law if we are to understand its purposes and change the law to fit new circumstances. Many legal rights arise from arguments over morality and justice, as is clear from the history of civil rights in America.

In every known society, rights are generated by rules regulating kinship, ritual, hunting, agriculture, land use, the distribution of resources, and much else. Families and clans may benefit more than individuals, but within the group we usually find some recognition of individual rights. Rights, then, are necessary building blocks of a social order. Because we cannot do without rights, it makes no sense to counterpose rights and community. No friend of community can be indifferent to rights or opposed to rights. Rather, communitarians are careful to distinguish among *kinds* of rights. They ask how rights are limited as well as protected, and they seek to balance the rights of individuals or groups against the needs of whole communities. This vindication of rights does not, by itself, make for a culture of rights-centeredness.

A rights-centered mentality arises from the fear that, in pursuit of the common good, short shrift might be given to the special needs and rightful claims of a community's members. Therefore, in contemporary liberal theory rights are "taken seriously," in Ronald Dworkin's phrase,[2] by giving them a special status or priority. In this view, rights are limits placed on political decisions. The underlying idea is that society should protect whatever has "intrinsic" worth—that is, whatever is valued for itself as an end, and not only as a means to other ends. Individual persons have intrinsic worth, and so do values or ideals, such as parental love and freedom of speech. Many social policies have to do with means rather than ends, such as the best or

---

2. See Ronald Dworkin, *Taking Rights Seriously* (Cambridge: Harvard University Press, 1978), pp. xi, 92.

most economical way of protecting the environment, educating children, or regulating business. Nevertheless, policy choices often put rights at risk, as when the lake behind a new dam floods land held sacred by a local or aboriginal community. These concerns are relieved, to some extent, when people challenge administrative decisions by invoking rights guaranteed by law. This may mean only that the interests of local communities may not be sacrificed without careful attention to their special interests and without appropriate compensation or mitigation of harm. So if we say rights are "trumps," we do not necessarily mean they cannot be limited, revised, or even extinguished.

Rights do not have equal claims to respect and protection. After all, some rights are generated by power, not justice. Therefore, we need to decide which rights are founded in justice, which are truly "basic," "fundamental," or "unalienable." Constitutional principles do much of this work. In the U.S. Constitution, freedom of speech and assembly, separation of church and state, and equal protection of the laws are among the principles that limit what government can do in the interests of efficiency or its understanding of the common good. As the American experience has shown, the work of constitution making is unending. Fundamental or not, rights must be understood in the light of historical changes, including opportunities as well as limiting circumstances. The original Bill of Rights was not meant to protect rights of all kinds, but only rights derived from what had been learned about civic participation in a democracy: what abuses of power must be guarded against, which personal choices must be respected, what kinds of controversy must be accepted and what kinds avoided.

Invoking Rights Responsibly. Duties tell us what we should do or must do, as parents, employees, or citizens. Rights are less compelling: they need not be claimed or asserted, and they may be waived or negotiated. Furthermore, there is a vital difference between invoking rights out of a sense of duty, or out of concern for the rights of others, and doing so to serve a narrow self-interest. We assert rights responsibly when we take account of consequences, especially consequences for social harmony and cooperation. A rights-centered mentality is indifferent to cooperation, which accommodates interests and seeks a shared commitment to ideals and purposes. We see this clearly in family life, where rights-centeredness signals breakdown or immaturity. In the latter case, it is supposed that someone else (parents and older siblings) will take care of the family's need for a spirit of reconciliation and strategies of cooperation. When a family is in good order, rights are not lost or forgotten, but they remain in the background, behind the scene, not in the foreground or at the center of family life. This means they are invoked sparingly and are subject to adjustment in the light of changing needs and circumstances. When a family breaks down, rights are more likely to be invoked.[3]

In public affairs, rights-centeredness produces social division, stalemate, and distorted priorities. Arguments based on rights do not count costs, promote accommodation, or care much about the purposes in view or the other values at stake.[4]

THE LURE OF ABSOLUTES

In a vigorous and subtle concurring opinion, Justice John Paul Stevens called attention to what he termed "the allure of absolute principles."[5] This temptation is a steady source of moral, legal, and political confusion. It is a very common way of doing evil in the name of the good; it is the devil to be wrestled with as we try to make moral judgments in principled ways.

Rights are not easily understood as nuanced and limited when they are considered sacred or when they become weapons in political combat. So-called "fundamental" rights, such as freedom of expression, are likely to be perceived as unconditional and nonnegotiable. They become part of a world taken for granted, whose premises are accepted unconsciously, without reflection. We often forget that the great spokesmen for rights, such as Thomas Jefferson, mostly knew, but could not always say, that each right eloquently proclaimed has a penumbra of understood meanings and unspoken qualifications.

3. Jeremy Waldron, "When Justice Replaces Affection: The Need for Rights," in *Liberal Rights: Collected Papers 1981–1991* (Cambridge: Cambridge University Press, 1993).

4. The costs of rights-centeredness are explored in Robert A. Kagan, *Adversarial Legalism: The American Way of Law* (Cambridge, Mass.: Harvard University Press, 2001).

5. *R.A.V. v. City of St. Paul, Minnesota*, 505 U.S. 377, 417 (1992).

The rhetorical imperative runs roughshod over nice differences and complex interpretations. The assumption is that only the simplicity of absolutes will stoke the fires of public opinion.

I have no wish to disparage rhetoric or deny the power of pithy slogans. We cannot insist on precision and subtlety when the task is to overcome complacency or win hearts and minds for righteous causes. The case is different, however, when we have to make sound moral judgments or devise workable rules in the light of facts as well as principles, or when we have reason to worry about the bad effects of glittering generalities or ideological thinking on our ability to resolve conflicts in creative ways. Ideological thinking prizes purity and coherence over patient concern for diverse interests, purposes, and values. Ideologues demand simplified alternatives, encourage a divide between "the children of light and the children of darkness," invite coercion in the name of correct doctrine. All this is alien to the spirit of community, which prefers the untidy concreteness of social existence to the comforts of political correctness.

A conspicuous example of taking rights too seriously by treating them as absolutes is the ardent defense of private property. Since the seventeenth century, most famously in the writings of John Locke, rights of private property have been celebrated as foundations of liberty, prosperity, and the rule of law. Earlier conceptions of property were more closely tied to kinship, inheritance, and limited land tenure. In modern times ownership and its prerogatives became more individualist and more market-oriented. The legal imagination was captured by Locke's compelling image of lonely, resolute, pioneering man, appropriating objects through toil, thereby uniting possession and selfhood. This doctrine became a major theme in the emerging culture of capitalism. It created and justified an ethos of domination, based on the premise that an owner can do as he likes with his own. There occurred a fateful "intellectual passage from the conception of private property as secondary and contingent to the conception of it as ultimate and absolute."[6] In American history the greatest evil spawned by this ethos was the slaveholder's claim that his property rights in chattel slavery could not be abridged.

There is indeed a close connection between private property and

---

6. Henry Scott Holland, "Property and Personality," in *Property: Its Duties and Rights*, edited by Charles Gore (London: Macmillan, 1915), p. 181.

liberty, security, opportunity, and prosperity. It does not follow, however, that all kinds of private property are equally worthy of protection, or that the virtues of private property are incompatible with responsible forms of ownership and control.

In fact, property rights are routinely limited in many ways. People who own property are accountable for the injuries or damage they cause; assets and earnings are taxed; land use is regulated. Although we take these limits for granted, the lure of absolutes is strong. A dream of unfettered ownership lingers in the modern mind, especially where no definite harm is done to particular persons or their property. As a result, it is difficult to control the building of homes on fragile coastlines, which are subject to severe storms and erosion, despite public costs and environmental damage. An absolutist conception of private property has long frustrated realistic policies affecting a wide range of issues, from gun control to the rights of shareholders in modern, publicly held corporations.

When the claims of private property are moderated, we can make more rational public policies, free of distortion by seductive imagery and rhetorical overreaching. We can attend to the public costs of protecting rights;[7] we can more wisely decide what limits on rights can be accepted without serious interference with legitimate activities.

Free Speech. The lure of absolutes has been especially strong among defenders of free speech. As in the case of private property, we too often misconstrue why we prize the rights in question and what must be done to protect them. In the United States, freedom of speech is guaranteed by the First Amendment's command that "Congress shall make no law . . . abridging the freedom of speech."[8] A complex jurisprudence has evolved, mostly in the twentieth century, damaged by a widespread view that almost any form of public expression counts as "speech" for purposes of First Amendment protection. Only the strictest scrutiny and the most stringent restrictions will offset an original sin we must attribute to all government—the wish to curb free speech in the interests of political stability and conventional morality. From this point of view, almost any utterance can be

7. Stephen Holmes and Cass R. Sunstein, *The Cost of Rights: Why Liberty Depends on Taxes* (New York: W. W. Norton, 1999).

8. For "Congress" we may now read "government," because under the Fourteenth Amendment (1868) the main provisions of the Bill of Rights were extended to the state governments.

thought to have constitutional value. This conclusion is more true of popular liberalism than of law because U.S. constitutional law does recognize important distinctions and limitations. But the rhetoric of free speech, even in judicial opinions, encourages the view that all speech is morally equivalent and that any regulation is dangerous or oppressive.

The strain toward absolutism in popular liberalism is supported by the writings of some liberal theorists. According to Ronald Dworkin, for example, the constitutional mandate cannot be understood or justified if we consider only the "instrumental" worth of free speech—that is, its contribution to political democracy or its usefulness in restraining the abuse of power. Rather, free speech has intrinsic worth, derived from the premise that all adults, except any who are mentally incompetent, must be treated as responsible moral agents. According to Dworkin, responsible moral agents rightly "insist on making up their own minds about what is good or bad in politics, or what is true or false in matters of justice or faith." Their dignity is violated if opinions are withheld from them on the ground that they are not fit to consider them. Further, they have a compelling desire to express their convictions to others—a desire that must be honored if their integrity as moral agents is to be respected.[9]

Here the idea of moral agency is overworked. Moreover, Dworkin's postulates are hardly self-evident. It is just as easy to suppose that responsible moral agents, for their own good reasons, may wish to defer to the authority of others, including the authority of a tradition, rather than make up their own minds, even on vital issues. And the desire for self-expression is highly variable, to say the least. More important than these overreachings, however, is the notion that we can draw specific conclusions about freedom of speech from a general theory of moral responsibility. We cannot know what it means to be responsible apart from knowing what it means to be a good citizen, a good physician, a good journalist, a good teacher, a good student. We are asked to draw from general concepts of responsibility or authority the conclusion that any censorship on grounds of content is unjustified.

Dworkin is surely right to say that freedoms of speech and ex-

9. Ronald Dworkin, "The Coming Battle over Free Speech," *New York Review of Books*, June 11, 1992.

pression have intrinsic worth. This means, first, that such freedoms are prized, not only for the social benefits they bring but also for their direct contributions to personal well-being; and second, that they have the capacity to sustain and enrich a wide range of values.[10]

Uncoerced communication is necessary for intellectual, emotional, and moral growth, and freedom of speech is valuable for many purposes, including science and education, as well as self-government.

FIDELITY TO CONTEXT

To make sense of rights—all but the most basic or "human" rights—we must understand the contexts within which their meanings are made clear and their claims are justified. Fidelity to context takes account of the distinctive purposes and values, as well as the constraints and opportunities, we find in particular human settings. Freedom and self-realization have different meanings—and different limits—in politics, religion, business, education, family life, and interaction in public places. The context tells us what kinds of liberty, creativity, or discipline are appropriate. We cannot apply what John Dewey called "the method of intelligence" without discovering how contexts affect ideals, or abstract models of motivation and conduct. Contextual thinking is not the enemy of ideals and principles; it is what makes them effective.

Political Speech. Where the lure of absolutes is strong, as in controversy over free speech, fidelity to context is hard to maintain. Democracy calls for robust expression of differing views regarding policies, candidates, and other public figures. In the interests of political freedom, we accept much that is inconvenient, offensive, and potentially dangerous. We endure the politics of distortion and deception. The special context of public discourse tells us that people should be free to speak their minds even if what they say is outrageous or revolutionary.

The context governs here as well. To protect political freedom we must understand its boundaries, including what should count as

---

10. Like many such dichotomies, the contrast between "instrumental" and "intrinsic" is not hard and fast. Ultimately, values are tested by their consequences, and in that sense are instrumental, but that does not mean they are *narrowly* instrumental.

political speech. Not all speech is political. Advertising products is
a kind of speech, but it is not political speech, and truth in advertising is properly regulated to protect consumers and competitors. Nor
does freedom of speech extend to making false and defamatory state-
ments about people who are not officials or "public figures." In the
interests of baseline morality, hardcore pornography is not protected.
Public discourse has its own integrity, its own standards, which must
be protected but also distinguished from standards we apply to other,
less valued forms of expression.

In honoring the First Amendment we bind ourselves to endure
abominable speech, such as racist speech.[11] We can and must distinguish abominable speech from abominable acts, even if the latter are
mainly intended to affect public opinion. We forbid and punish beat-
ing homosexuals, burning churches, or murdering abortion doctors,
even though such acts express ideas and attitudes. Burning a cross at
someone's home is expressive, to be sure, but it may also be treated
as a criminal assault. Public discourse must be open to new forms
of expression, including demonstrative acts as well as words, but that
does not save us from the need to distinguish peaceful picketing and
some forms of trespass, such as the sit-in tactics of the civil rights
movement, from violent acts of terror or personal intimidation.

Academic Freedom. The schools and universities of a free society
are an especially revealing context for understanding rights. Academic freedom fosters open discussion and free inquiry, untrammeled
by rules that suppress debate, enforce orthodoxies, cramp creativity,
or retard innovation. Individual self-expression is encouraged, and
much eccentricity is tolerated. Nevertheless, the main objective is
better learning, teaching, and research. In academic freedom, the
rights of individuals are derivative—that is, they stem from and are
justified by the institution's distinctive aims and competencies. Individual rights are recognized because in that way a common good is
advanced.

The point is to create a free community of learning. The sovereignty of purpose and of institutional ideals establishes the limits
of freedom as well as its reach. All schools have rules regulating con-

11. Adolf Hitler's *Mein Kampf* may be freely sold in the United States, though it
is banned in Germany. Still, as a community we may properly oppose such ideas,
and we may do so in tax-supported ways, such as public education. Furthermore,
freedom of speech does not require equal time, or any allocated time, for all ideas.

duct in the classroom, the content of the curriculum, and the authority of teachers. In these rules the content of speech is governed, as is the "time, place, and manner" of public expression.[12] Students are routinely required to speak or write on assigned topics. They must meet standards of thought and relevance. When professors publish research, their work is judged according to accepted criteria of good scholarship and science. The curriculum is selective and does not pretend to give every idea an opportunity to be heard or taught. The biological sciences exclude creationism, and do so with an easy conscience. In short, academic freedom is a form of *ordered* liberty.

Contexts and Principles. Fidelity to context is not a flight from principle, nor does it presume that every human situation is different. Fidelity to context is a way of determining rights and realizing values, in the light of governing purposes and exigent circumstances. Contextual thinking improves judgment by ensuring that all relevant values are considered and by avoiding excessive reliance on abstract, unsituated conceptions, such as "rationality," "equality," "autonomy," and "moral agency." Without specifying contexts, we cannot really say what these ideals are supposed to accomplish or how to achieve them.

We should reject the temptation to overstress the uniqueness of events and decisions.[13] Instead, we can learn how to classify situations in helpful ways. Values like free speech, privacy, autonomy, and respect for others have different meanings, limits, and opportunities, in family life, democratic politics, journalism, higher education, the legal profession, and military organization. Close study of these and other contexts yields principles of right conduct, which we may look to for guidance in designing institutions and in making decisions. Ultimately, of course, every situation is unique, and each makes its own demands for sensitive judgment. But that is no bar to the quest for principles that bring values to bear within contexts we understand or can learn to understand.

12. In December 1964 the Academic Senate of the University of California at Berkeley adopted a resolution that stated in part: "The content of speech or advocacy should not be restricted by the University." Although stated in general terms, the resolution took for granted a context of public discourse on campus. It was not meant to govern rules regulating what students should write or say in class or in their assignments.

13. For a different view see Stanley Fish, *The Trouble with Principle* (Cambridge, Mass.: Harvard University Press, 1999).

RELATIVISM AND HUMAN RIGHTS

When "human rights" are in question, we encounter the claims of moral and cultural relativism. The appeal of relativism is strong, but a global ethic, which upholds human rights, is far from alien to the communitarian persuasion. The experience of community, as I have noted before, looks outward as well as inward. It does so, however, without slighting the benefits of diversity and of local attachments.

The term *human rights* distinguishes rights that are special and subject to change, such as citizenship, marriage, property, or contract, from rights that belong to all human beings just because they are human. Human rights may or may not be recognized by government or even by custom. All legal systems uphold some human rights—for example, a right to be protected from unjustified violence. Law steps in to define the offenses more precisely, determine guilt or innocence, and provide for penalties and defenses. In this process the underlying human rights are vindicated but not thereby created. This understanding gives us moral leverage to criticize the law, and change it, when human rights are violated, weakly protected, or dimly perceived.

At bottom, what we take to be human rights must reflect what we know about human nature and the human condition. This knowledge is refined and tested to take account of differences in history and culture. But the lessons of history and anthropology do not foreclose generalizations about humanity. Indeed, American anthropologists of the 1930s who did much to advance cultural relativism were nevertheless keen to establish what they called the "psychic unity of mankind."[14] They sought recognition of a common humanity whose peoples, despite great differences, are worthy of respect and fellowship. They pointed to an array of characteristically human needs, dispositions, and emotions, such as pride, self-respect, and arrogance; the universality of aesthetic impulses; a rich symbolic experience. They wanted humanity to be understood as biologically One and culturally Many. This premise made possible empathetic understanding of very different expressions of the human spirit.

---

14. For background see "Plurality and Relativism," *The Moral Commonwealth* (Berkeley: University of California Press, 1992), chap. 4.

Cultural relativism has been a strong voice for human rights: respect for cultural differences, rights of cultural membership and identity, the right of an indigenous culture to survive, not only for the sake of those who are nourished by it, but as part of a common human heritage. This point of view can be called responsible relativism, but it is not necessarily a radical relativism. Because radical relativism denied or misunderstood the psychic unity of mankind and disparaged "cultural universals," it was repudiated, as mistaken and incoherent, by such leading anthropologists as Clyde Kluckhohn and Robert Redfield. We should understand what they had to say, and follow their lead. Human rights derive from the secure foundations everyone needs to live a vulnerable life in the company of others.

The communitarian persuasion resists the temptation to think that any worthy ideal necessarily creates basic or human rights. We cannot respect diversity and also feel free to embrace (and impose) a single standard of belief, conduct, or institutional life. Because there are many different ways of being human, we cannot respect diversity and refuse to respect, within broad limits, different conceptions of religion, government, education, sexuality, child rearing, and kinship. We who believe in the equality of men and women, in the virtues of self-government, or in educational opportunity for all, may well argue that these ideals should be universally accepted. However, we cannot say that other ways of life, which deny these ideals or do not give them great weight, should therefore be condemned as morally reprehensible and beyond the pale.

Crimes against Humanity. The law of human rights takes its departure from a baseline morality. This is no more than conventional wisdom, which faithfully reflects the grim experience of the twentieth century. The greatly increased concern for human rights has been mainly a response to *atrocities*. As defined by the Charter of the International Military Tribunal, "crimes against humanity" include "murder, extermination, enslavement, deportation, and other inhumane acts."[15]

Crimes against humanity are great afflictions, which no social goals can excuse. In these cases, there can be no appeal to moral or cultural relativism. The victims are not an abstract "humanity."

15. Article 6, Charter of the International Military Tribunal, in Agreement for the Prosecution and Punishment of the Major War Criminals of the European Axis, August 8, 1945, 82 UNTS 279, 286–288.

They are particular persons being tortured, murdered, or enslaved. The oppressed are known to all and to themselves. The oppressors hide their crimes or justify them in ways no morally sensitive community can accept.

In this chapter we have seen that communitarian thought gives effect to rights while upholding an ethic of responsibility. Claims of rights are suspect when they are driven by narrow self-interest; when they are uninformed by the values to be realized in particular contexts; when they are asserted without regard for costs and tradeoffs; and when rights are divorced from obligations, including the duty to enhance cooperation by finding common ground and reconciling competing interests. Social life depends on recognizing rights, as we do in a marriage and in contracts of all sorts, but the welfare of a family or business is not well served by a preoccupation with rights. People who care only or even mainly about their rights are not good models for cooperation, to say nothing of fellowship. We must sometimes stand apart, as dreamers, prophets, or whistle-blowers. However, our normal lives are lived with others. We cannot live interdependent lives if we believe "getting our rights" should be our main concern. Moreover, we cannot know what rights we should have without an understanding of the common good. The rights of citizens, employees, landowners, students, or parents are not given by revelation or determined once and for all. The American Declaration of Independence speaks of "unalienable rights" and says that *among these* are "life, liberty, and the pursuit of happiness." The Declaration does not provide us with a complete list of unalienable rights, and those mentioned, though rhetorically powerful, are comfortably vague. It is left for the community to decide what rights are to be protected, and in what ways. The federal Constitution drafted in 1787 drew inspiration from the Declaration of 1776, but it also invoked a special history of "the rights of Englishmen."

If we ask for fidelity to context, and to the common good, we do so not to disparage rights but to give them their proper place within a moral, political, and legal order. It is our shared experience of the abuse of power, and of the conditions that make for security, cooperation, and the release of energies, that leads us to treasure civil liberty, parental authority, private property and much else that cannot be understood without the language of rights. That same experience tells us, however, that abstract, unsituated rights are poor guides to moral judgment and social policy. The communitarian critique reminds us that rights belong within and not outside the experience of collective life; within and not outside thoughtful concern for the fabric of society.

CHAPTER 7

DEMOCRACY MADE GOOD

WE THE PEOPLE

The past century has seen many travesties of democracy, many tyrannies cloaked in the symbolism of popular rule. Adolf Hitler came to power by popular election, and he confirmed his authority by plebiscites and mass rallies. Communist regimes have been called "people's democracies" and "democratic republics." These experiences have driven home the lesson that democracy cannot be equated with "consent of the governed." Rather, democracy—literally "rule by the people"—requires *self-preserving* consent. This means, first, that consent is revocable. There can be no question of creating a self-perpetuating regime on the basis of a single election or plebiscite. Second, consent is self-preserving when the process allows sustained criticism of authority, which requires protection of individual and minority rights. It is a parody of democracy, a crude mockery of its ideals and purposes, when democratic forms are relied on to justify or sustain authoritarian or totalitarian regimes.

Revocable and self-preserving consent is implicit in the argument of the Declaration of Independence. There "consent of the governed" is coupled with an affirmation of "unalienable rights." If a government abuses its powers by violating those rights, it forfeits consent and can be replaced, if necessary by revolution.

Who are "the people"? How do they act? The whole community

is meant, not just a part, and the people act through institutions that can claim widespread respect. Democracy is made good when collective decisions are based on the participation of all legitimate groups and interests, and when a written or unwritten constitution governs the making and execution of laws and public policies. It follows that genuine democracy cannot be wholly committed to majority rule. Some restraints on majority rule must be accepted.

Majority rule is best understood as a method by which the people as a whole are represented. In any numerous decision-making body, some procedure is needed for coming to a decision, and majority rule is very often expedient and satisfactory. The alternatives are stalemate or granting too much power to an official or a committee. However, majority rule can be cumbersome, unreliable, and overly divisive. We may want a stronger consensus than a bare majority can provide. A bare majority may not always be accepted as the legitimate voice of the whole body or people. Therefore, we turn to supermajorities, as in rules requiring more than a majority for approval of local taxation or constitutional amendment. We also rely on nonmajoritarian institutions, such as the Supreme Court, or devices such as the presidential veto, to check the will of majorities.

If the people are sovereign, they are so not as detached individuals, but as associated participants in a living community. They act collectively in and through their traditions and institutions, in and through taken-for-granted understandings and attachments. In a democracy the people are, we believe, the safest repositories of ultimate political authority. That faith is challenged when community decays.

As an expression of the will of the people, majority rule is neither sure nor self-sufficient. It is not sure because it may fall well short of consensus and must be supplemented by super-majorities; it is not self-sufficient because democracy calls for procedures that make it possible for minorities to become majorities. A current majority cannot be allowed to oppress minorities or to curb their opportunities for debate and succession.

DELIBERATION AND COMMUNITY

The American founders wanted government to be republican as well as democratic. The will of the people would be sovereign. Yet two nagging questions remained: How is the will of the people to be ascertained? And how should that will be governed? These questions reflected the view that popular sovereignty cannot be equated with action based on undisciplined passion or foreshortened vision. Democratic will, like any human will, must be tempered by reason and nourished by virtue. Reason requires orderly process and prudential judgment, which takes account of multiple values, informing contexts, and unintended effects. Virtue calls for a morally aware electorate, and for leaders who can resist the temptations of power, pride, and unjust enrichment.

The remedy is "deliberative democracy," which recalls the classical view that pure democracy is at best unstable and at worst a recipe for disorder and tyranny. The founders envisioned a "democratic republic" capable of "reconciling the advantages of democracy with the sobering qualities of republicanism."[1] These qualities include the "republican virtue" of commitment to the common good— a virtue that democracy as such need not embrace. The will of the people can be misdirected, manipulated, or self-destructive.

Deliberative democracy depends on "people in community." It presumes the existence of a shared ethos governing political controversy, and an array of appropriate and competent institutions. Deliberative democracy allows people-in-community to reason together and act collectively. Democracy is not primarily a way of managing diversity. The point is to mobilize energies for sound policies. Democratic government is purposive and problem-solving. Diverse interests and divergent outlooks are accommodated, but democracy is not paralyzed by the specter of warring gods.

Nor is deliberative democracy mainly a way of registering preferences or choosing among competing elites. Deliberation leads naturally to the criticism of preferences, as when we learn from experience that gas-guzzling motor vehicles deplete resources and damage the environment. Collective intelligence cannot take preferences as given and unchangeable.

---

1. Martin Diamond, Winston Mills Fisk, and Herbert Garfinkel, *The Democratic Republic: An Introduction to American National Government* (Chicago: Rand McNally, 1966), p. xi. Winston Churchill once remarked in Parliament, "No one pretends that democracy is perfect or all-wise. Indeed, it has been said that democracy is the worst form of government. Except all those other forms that have been tried from time to time" (*Hansard*, November 11, 1947, col. 206).

These perspectives build democracy into the fabric of community. A supportive ethic of responsibility guards against deception and demagogic appeals. In direct democracy political decisions are often self-defeating because they are detached from contexts that regulate opinion and channel decisions. For example, when we try to legislate by popular referendum, voters are asked to weigh and decide complex issues, which should receive more careful, more consultative, more filtered scrutiny. Opportunities for deception abound.[2] Paradoxically, the influence of well-organized, well-financed groups is magnified rather than diminished.

Free Speech and Campaign Reform. The interest in reforming election campaigns to control the access and power that money can buy is driven by a confident belief in the corrupting effects of greatly increased costs in election campaigns. These costs produce an intense preoccupation with fund raising. The proposed reforms have been attacked as offensive to free speech and barred by the First Amendment. This controversy has brought home the significance of understanding democracy as a deliberative process. Deliberative democracy invites and justifies the careful design of institutions. Facts as well as values must be assessed, including necessary tradeoffs among different rights and competing duties. We must also consider how debate is carried on and how public policy is made. Majorities are not wholly free to make these judgments, for they are bound down by the Constitution. However, the Constitution does not bar fresh thought as to which claims of right are truly fundamental and must be honored, and which may give way without serious damage to underlying ideals.

Like the broader idea of reason, deliberation encompasses many kinds of debate and inquiry, including sometimes painful scrutiny of our own preconceptions. It would be wrong to suppose that deliberation is necessarily cool, untouched by sharp disagreements or tense confrontation. As in the civil rights struggle led by Martin Luther King Jr. in the 1960s, a strategy of confrontation can reveal the unresponsiveness of law and politics, the frustration and unrest behind a façade of social peace, and the reserves of support that may exist for new

2. On the California experience with popular referenda, see Peter Schrag, *Paradise Lost* (New York: New Press, 1998).

policies and new ways of thinking. Without confrontation, unspoken assumptions may be insulated from criticism. Interests hitherto unvoiced—those of women, minorities, the poor—may remain unheard. Deliberative democracy encourages openness by enlarging opportunities for civic participation and by providing appropriate safeguards against deception and manipulation. We need to examine and re-examine the democracy we have and the special problems it creates. The ills of democracy are likely to reveal the ills of community.

SELF-GOVERNMENT AND BUREAUCRACY

An especially insidious challenge to self-government is the so-called "problem of bureaucracy." A community cannot act collectively—cannot even define its own interests and purposes—without delegating authority to officials and agencies. In this respect democracy shares the fate of all complex organizations. Delegation is unavoidable, yet in all organizations it endangers integrity and control. As an organization grows in complexity, new interests are created, goals are deflected, policies are distorted. These outcomes can be offset but not eliminated. That is no counsel of despair, still less a justification for rejecting government. Rather, the problem of bureaucracy is a challenge to intelligence. The appropriate response is thoughtful diagnosis, sustained experiment, and hopeful reform.

In ordinary usage, and in much social science as well, bureaucracy is condemned and even despised. Negative images of rigid hierarchy, rule-bound administration, protected turf, and organizational rivalry are evoked. Visions are conjured up of expanded powers and bigger budgets, administered by inflexible, insensitive, unresponsive officials. Yet bureaucracy is also appreciated. Compared to an officialdom chosen on the basis of family connections, class privilege, or political patronage, modern bureaucracy is far more rational, objective, honest, and purposive. Indeed, a career civil service, which rewards education, merit, and fidelity to law, is a proven pillar of modern government. The same may be said of the large corporation. Wall Street expects family-owned firms with publicly traded shares to install professional managers and corporate bureaucracies. In these and similar contexts bureaucrats are simply officials to whom authority is delegated by boards of directors or elected leaders. Therefore, a modern dictionary can say of bureaucracy that it is "administration of government through bureaus staffed with nonelective officials."[3] Bureaucracy is an accepted and dominant feature of the social landscape.

The pathologies of bureaucracy are, to a large extent, unwanted byproducts of its distinctive virtues. Upholding rules and protecting a special mission or competence are virtues that encourage the characteristic drawbacks of bureaucracy: rules, policies, and precedents become sacrosanct; authority is husbanded, rather than risked and shared; official lines of communication are too eagerly defended; cooperation is sacrificed to organizational rivalry; routine is rewarded, initiative discouraged. Most important is a disposition to protect "the system," which thus comes to matter more than individual persons or even the organization's purposes or goals. A weakened sense of purpose helps produce complacent bureaucrats and unresponsive government.

The failings of bureaucracy are a chief subject matter for the science of administration, which studies both public and private bureaucracy. Rational administration has costs and flaws, but that is no reason to condemn it or to try to do without it. We do not give up physical exercise because it may be harmful as well as beneficial, scholarship because many of its products seem dry and academic, law because it may degenerate into "legalism." Exercise, scholarship, and law are goods, not evils, even if they need sensible guidelines and practical compromises.

Reinventing Bureaucracy. Social scientists and creative administrators have greatly improved our ability to diagnose, resist, and overcome the weaknesses of bureaucracy. Modern "postbureaucratic" organization rejects top-down, "command and control" approaches to discipline, initiative, coordination, and communication. The aim is to promote more flexible, more purposive, more problem-centered ways of mobilizing human energies for effective (and cost-effective) action. Cooperation is the ideal, consultation is the keynote, initiative is the prize.

These changes in theory and practice do not signal an end to bureaucracy. They do not do away with authority, or officially defined goals, or the need for standing rules, official communication, expertise, planning, and the division of labor. Under attack is the received ethos of bureaucracy, with its preference for fixed hierarchies

3. *American Heritage Dictionary*, 3rd ed. Note that in this definition bureaucracy is a feature of private as well as public government.

and centralized command. In the postbureaucratic model, many bureaucratic pathologies are recognized and corrected, but the imperatives of leadership, discipline, and impersonal judgment remain. We can reform bureaucracy but we cannot do without it.

The new theories of administration have mainly centered on the internal life of large organizations, especially how to improve services, innovation, and morale. In the larger democratic community, however, self-government calls for more than improved initiative and morale. Reforming bureaucracy centers on making government more *transparent, accessible,* and *open to criticism.*

Transparency is a fancy word for openness. Decisions are made visible to all concerned, and so are premises taken for granted, alternatives considered or ignored, alliances made and unmade, ideas treated seriously or dismissed. Visibility provides leverage for criticism. Other perspectives are brought to the table, and procedures can be questioned when there is reason to believe they are unwise, illegal, or unfair.

These principles are well established in American administrative law, which is the law of public bureaucracy. Early in the twentieth century, with the expansion of government regulation by the Interstate Commerce Commission, the Federal Trade Commission, and many other agencies, much concern was expressed that government officials might act arbitrarily. These concerns led to many restrictions on official conduct, especially in the regulation of business. The Administrative Procedure Act of 1946 recognized that agencies issuing rules regulating private conduct, and creating or limiting private rights, are engaged in law making. Therefore, they should be subject to appropriate standards of fairness and due process. The new administrative law greatly expanded public participation by requiring notice of proposed regulations, and opportunities for the public to be heard. As a result, government agencies are more open to scrutiny. They must include in their deliberations a broader range of interests and concerns.

These reforms deflate the pretensions of bureaucracy, especially a claim that "expertise" can be wholly relied on to determine the public interest. Instead, the law recognizes that official decisions can be unduly limited by unspoken assumptions about which interests or purposes are worthy and which can be ignored, and by unexamined beliefs about everything from what makes for efficient management to conceptions of nature, exploitation, and conservation. In the new dispensation, these assumptions can be brought to light and questioned. Officials are asked to listen and learn.

Furthermore, the line between government and civil society is blurred. Officials do not act alone, with confidence in the legitimacy of their commands. They must accept one or another form of shared governance, which calls for wider participation in forming, implementing, and monitoring policy. Shared governance enriches communication, encourages collaboration, and seeks consensus.

As a remedy for bureaucratic rigidity and pretense, this turn toward a measure of participatory democracy is full of promise. Yet a perilous downside cannot be ignored. In practice the most articulate and powerful interests come to stand for "the people," yet they may be highly unrepresentative, and the polices they advocate may run counter to the public interest.

This is the Achilles' heel of open, responsive government. It is what James Madison called the evil of "faction," and what is known today as the pernicious influence of "special interests." The remedy lies in a better understanding of responsive government. "Responsiveness" is not self-serving opportunism, nor is it weakness in the face of pressure. A genuinely responsive institution holds fast to its animating principles and distinctive purposes. At the same time, it is prepared to listen, learn, and change its ways as new circumstances arise and new voices are heard. In other words, a responsive institution is able to adapt without compromising its core commitments. A government welfare program is responsive if it maintains fidelity to an ethos of caring, and to its role as part of a social safety net; if its policies show respect for the genuine problems of the poor, including their need for productive work and a sense of responsibility and self-worth; and if it is willing and ready to listen to those who speak for their clients and future clients.

Responsiveness cannot be effective without a professional bureaucracy, staffed by officials who can create and transmit an appropriate organizational culture. The trick is to combine institutional self-confidence with strategies of outreach and a spirit of self-correction.

THE COMMUNITARIAN CULTURE OF DEMOCRACY

A barebones democracy (with reasonably free elections and basic civil rights) may be hastily put together or imposed from without, even sustained for a time, with tanks and bayonets. (Haiti and Bosnia are recent examples.) A more robust democracy is embedded in a culture from which it draws vitality and strength. I call this culture communitarian because it consists of beliefs, practices, traditions, and institutions, which together create a covenanted people, committed to the ideals and shared understandings that make self-government possible, rewarding, and self-sustaining. In such a culture, self-interest is moderated, cooperation is encouraged, and the reality of interdependence is acknowledged and reinforced.

Education for Civic Virtue. The most important gift of culture to democracy is the formation of persons who accept the values of self-government, including toleration, trust, and criticism. Like any culture, the culture of democracy is an offspring of community, especially the experience of growing up in families and schools. In these settings, if all goes well, the virtues of fellowship, responsibility, and citizenship are fostered. Hence there is a vital public interest in how children are brought up and in the quality of schools and other socializing agencies. The ensuing tension is irrepressible. In an effective democracy schools should be significantly autonomous. Yet the political system cannot be indifferent to their success or failure. It matters what attitudes and values are transmitted, even when what the schools teach is otherwise good. In a culture of democracy, education is not limited to learning specialized skills, nor can it be cabined by ethnic, religious, or local perspectives. If they care about civic virtue, schools must pay attention to children as whole persons, including their capacity for moral awareness, self-restraint, and cooperation—in a word, their character. This imperative affects curriculum, teaching, the nature of the school community, and public policies for the organization of school systems or the integration of public and private education.

Democracy and Diversity. In chapter 4, I examined the idea of "a unity of unities." This "federal principle," I suggested, is a fundamental tenet of the communitarian persuasion. It is especially important for understanding democracy, which requires respectful regard for the particular persons, groups, practices, and institutions that together form society. In a democracy we take for granted that there will be diverse interests and contending outlooks. This diversity is not a troublesome noise, to be silenced by a central authority. Rather, it is a prime source of energy and creativity.

The American motto, *E pluribus unum,* is perhaps only a reminder that the federal union was formed from originally separate states. A profounder meaning, however, is that *plurality within a comprehensive unity* remains a vital part of the nation's self-conception. Although the states are subordinate in many ways, they are also autonomous and endowed with intrinsic worth as agencies of self-government.

Limited and Responsive Government. Liberals and conservatives agree that a line must be drawn separating private and public concerns. Liberals think that individuals should be free to decide for themselves what to think and what to say, without being subject to public scrutiny or control. Conservatives think that the private realm, which encompasses family life, religion, and economic activity, should be mostly free from external control. Both want to limit paternalism and other authoritarian temptations.

Hardly anyone is against *some* government intrusion into private life, to protect public health and safety, educate the young, or conscript armies for defense. "Social conservatives" think government may and should enforce conventional morality; welfare liberals rely on government to provide a multitude of services while trying to protect clients who may be dependent or powerless. These differences tell us that the idea of limited government does not contain a sure guide to policy. Everything depends on how we understand the chief purposes of government and how we accommodate competing values.

A communitarian commitment to limited government is implicit in the idea of "a unity of unities." To protect the legitimate components of community, which include individual persons as well as groups and institutions, some bounds must be set on the reach and power of a central government. Limited government can and should be responsive as well, and this may call for blurred boundaries. Improving education or increasing the availability of affordable housing are problems that do not fall neatly into public or private spheres. They may call for combining private energies with the authority and resources of government.

Trust, Criticism, and the Rule of Law. In a democracy people act collectively but, as I have said, they do so in self-preserving ways. The balance is not easily struck. Collective life demands authority and obedience, while self-preservation inspires skepticism and distrust. Thomas Jefferson, who did not much like constitutional restraints on popular will, gave expression to this spirit of distrust when he said that "free government is founded in jealousy, and not in confidence;

it is jealousy, not confidence, which prescribes limited constitutions, to bind down those whom we are obliged to trust with power."[4]

Intensified by other historical currents, such as a strong tradition of individualism, the healthy distrust natural to democracy can become a threat to self-government. To avoid this outcome, we strive for a constructive union of trust and criticism. Trust is needed for all the ways in which we rely on one another for cooperation and self-restraint. Its troubling offspring is respect for authority. People gain a great deal from many kinds of subordination and deference. In functional families, churches, schools, and hospitals, respect for authority goes hand in hand with self-respect. Democracy is no exception. Political life suffers when widespread distrust encourages apathy and alienation. Yet, without criticism, trust endangers deliberative democracy. Critical inquiry keeps a close eye on the uses of power.

The union of trust and criticism lends nobility and strength to the rule of law, which is the indispensable framework for civic life. Democracy is wholly dependent on this framework, and fidelity to law is a virtue we ask of the governed as well as the governors, of citizens as well as officials. Obedience to law is a prima facie moral obligation. It is a presumption rebuttable in special situations of oppression and betrayal, but a presumption nonetheless. Even "civil disobedience," as understood by Mahatma Gandhi and Martin Luther King Jr., is nuanced and respectful. It is a form of protest that honors and extends a culture of lawfulness, even as it challenges laws and rebukes authority. Disobedience occurs within a steadying framework of trust and commitment.

A Culture of Renewal. Democracy requires a spirit of openness and an ethos of reconstruction. We need those values in part because we must deal collectively, in democratic ways, with a world in which new circumstances are forever creating new problems. Effective self-government is not nourished by cynicism and distrust. The optimistic attitude of American pragmatists, as in the influential writings of William James and John Dewey, was a fitting expression of the culture of democracy. For Dewey, democracy is above all a way of learning collectively how to resolve new and recurrent problems. He thought the culture of democracy was more important than its

---

4. Quoted from E. D. Warfield, *The Kentucky Resolutions of 1798* (New York: G. P. Putnam's, 1887), pp. 157–158.

forms. In this he sometimes went too far, but the point he made is still helpful and important.

Another imperative for effective democracy is the reconciliation of differences. Inclusion is the keynote, enriched by the understanding that diversity and disagreement are constant features of political life. For minorities to feel included, something more is wanted than the opportunity to debate, vote, and accept defeat. Within broad limits minorities should be able to pursue their interests and affirm their identities. They do so in part by participating in the refashioning of social attitudes and norms, such as those affecting race relations, gender differences, and sexual morality. So long as minorities meet threshold standards of acceptable conduct—standards that evolve but do not disappear—they should not be shut out from the community's work of self-determination. Thus, we return to the communitarian principle with which I began this chapter: "we the people" includes everyone, not just the majority.

CHAPTER 8

RESPONSIBLE ENTERPRISE

As I have said more than once, and in different ways, an ethos of responsibility is central to the communitarian vision. We have explored some of the ways in which responsibility is weakened by the realities of modernity, and by important strands of liberal thought. These trends affect social as well as personal responsibility. An especially important reality is the large, often multinational corporation. What are the moral and social responsibilities of this rough beast?

IDOLS OF THE MARKET

In what has been called the "market mentality" we find attitudes and assumptions that faithfully express but also distort the foundational assumptions of modern capitalism. In short, a market mentality leads to irresponsible conduct. To take a different path, we must first understand what is wrong with these assumptions.

New communitarians have no trouble appreciating capitalist institutions: private property and investment, free markets for the exchange of goods and services, competition as a spur to innovation and lower costs, energies released by entrepreneurial initiative. Capitalism has brought phenomenal advances in technology and prosperity, with all that means for the health, longevity, comfort, and education of large populations. This legacy is troubling, however, insofar as it encourages misplaced enthusiasm for applying free-market principles to all spheres of life while ignoring the social and political frameworks on which economic life depends. We cannot accept as necessary the harms unbridled capitalism can do to public health, the natural environment, and the quality of social life.

The chief failing of the market mentality is what I earlier called the lure of absolutes. The temptation is to transform an idea made reasonable by a tacit understanding of its limits into an idea corrupted by a lost sense of connectedness and restraint. I call these ideas "idols of the market" because they become, inappropriately, articles of faith and objects of worship.

Maximization. We often benefit from trying to attain the highest possible production, goals, profit margins, approval ratings, test scores, runs batted in, or yards gained in football scrimmage. Getting the most of what there is to get, given available resources, is a powerful incentive and a clear criterion of success.

But maximization loses focus when goals are subtle and imprecise, bundled with other goals, subject to compromise and tradeoffs. In education, for example, teaching and learning cannot be equated with preparation for tests or performance on tests. In sports, athletes must follow the rules, even if doing so lowers their scores. In business, profits are limited by legal rules, the need for cooperation, and at least some awareness of moral responsibility. To be sure, a business must be profitable or shut down. There is a great difference, however, between sustaining or enhancing profits, and *maximizing* them. If maximization is taken literally, as a sole guide to decision, it becomes an offense to prudence and good sense, which take for granted the need for rules and standards, and for tradeoffs imposed by technical, economic, or political necessities.

No enterprise can be part of a community without accepting limits on what it can do and how far it can go in pursuing its special objectives. It is always pertinent to ask how the pursuit of a particular goal affects other goals, values, and interests. This is the key to responsible conduct.

Property. As I noted in chapter 6, p. 72, the modern idea of property is individualist and market-centered. By the seventeenth century, an ideal of unfettered exchange was replacing traditional restrictions, such as the entailment of landed property to protect the rights of heirs. Market capitalism thrives on the free exchange of assets and commodities. Human services are perceived as units of labor, to be exchanged for wages, without considering the needs of persons or families. As markets and the market mentality expanded, what Karl Marx called "the fetishism of commodities" became apparent. "Commodification" transforms items of intrinsic worth into assets available for exchange at will. Yet the reins were not wholly loosened. Property rights have been (and are) limited in many ways. Different kinds of property are treated differently. Copyright and patent law establish temporary rights in ideas and writings; zoning laws govern the uses of land; a market for babies is prohibited. Regulation of business practice, affecting labor conditions, the sale of stocks and bonds, and much else, is routinely imposed and accepted. Nevertheless, despite these qualifications, the sibling idols of private property and free exchange exert a powerful influence on public policy. They frustrate the protection of important values from market forces.

In the history of thought about property there has long been a tension between property as person-centered and as market-centered. For John Locke, writing in the seventeenth century, property is created when individuals mix their labor with something tangible and thereby make it their own. In its most important form, private property is the ownership and control of one's own person. Locke thought of property as an incident of personhood, a pillar of independence, a resource for the nurture and protection of individuals and families. By the nineteenth century, however, property became a more market-centered idea, more impersonal and abstract. Every unit of property would be, in principle, readily interchangeable with other units, whose value was measured by what they would bring on the market.

This outcome has done much to encourage commerce, savings, investment, and the free flow of capital. Property rights bring security and flexibility to economic transactions, thus releasing energies and mobilizing resources. At the same time this abstract, unsituated conception of property has frustrated the quest for enterprise responsibility. This is so largely because the shareholders of a business corporation are its legal owners, and ownership carries rights of control, including the right to destroy the enterprise or merge it with another, regardless of consequences for other interests. A taken-for-granted association of ownership and control harks back to the person-centered conception of private property, which has retained its hold on the legal imagination, even though a great many shareholders are now transitory, uncommitted participants in a fluid market for corporate equities. Although the nature of investment has greatly changed, the significance of that change has not been faced. The union of ownership and control has been sanctified by an inappropriate and irrelevant imagery, which interferes with realistic assessments of all the stakeholders, including shareholders, whose interests merit protection.

Limited Obligation. I suggested in chapter 2 that the fundamental virtue of community is an ethos of open-ended obligation, and that this ethos is undermined by the modern idea of contract, which closely specifies what the parties undertake to do and when their obligations must be met. The market mentality comes into its own when people can know, as precisely as possible, just what responsibilities they have assumed. The principle of limited obligation runs into trouble when relationships are more permanent, as in a marriage, or when enduring organizations are created. The more we insist on limiting obligations, and making them predictable, the harder it is to establish trust or motivate people to do their best or to make sacrifices. Therefore, the contract model, as an aspect of the market mentality, is not a good guide to the design of effective institutions.[1]

Unreflective Choice. Markets exalt as well as register the preferences of consumers. What people want is the measure of value, and freedom of choice becomes a cultural icon; choice is valued for itself, not only as a fact of economic life. Respect for preferences is certainly necessary for rational decisions about investment, production, and marketing. But celebrating choice is much less defensible when the worth of what is produced, sold, or communicated cannot be measured solely by what people want or prefer. What is good for us or for the community cannot be dictated by consumer choice. People may choose to smoke, overeat, or drive inefficient vehicles; education is degraded if students or parents can decide what should be taught and how to teach. A constitutional government places many limits on what majorities can choose. The market mentality transforms a necessary respect for preference in, say, a market for shoes or pants, into a more absolute criterion, which should not apply when important values are placed at risk by short-sighted, self-indulgent, or unreflective preferences.

1. On the tension between contract and association, see my *Law, Society and Industrial Justice* (1969; reprint, New Brunswick, N.J.: Transaction Books, 1980), pp. 52–62. See also Oliver E. Williamson, *Markets and Hierarchies* (New York: Free Press, 1975).

THE INSTITUTIONAL IMPERATIVE

A first line of resistance to the market mentality is found in the natural history of institutions. A business enterprise or other organization may begin, in the minds of its founders, as a coolly rational and wholly controllable instrument for achieving predetermined purposes. Over time, however, the enterprise becomes a dense network of human relations, vested interests, and customary practices. Commitments are made to employees, clients, customers, investors, and a surrounding community. At a minimum, standards of law-abiding conduct must be met. Therefore, *who says organization says obligation.*[2]

Most obligations are useful and empowering. They open channels, mobilize energies, and foster cooperation. They also impose costs. As this tension-laden drama unfolds, organizations become institutions. A distinctive culture or character is created. This process, which we call "institutionalization," has many benefits. To a military organization it brings combat-readiness; to industry it brings quality control. Yet institutionalization can be disabling if, for example, racism, shoddy production, or corruption becomes part of an organization's way of life. The result may be what Veblen called a "trained incapacity" to reform or adapt.

Institutionalization, for good or ill, is the source of much concern among managers and leaders. The troubles are often hard to bear, and many managers would like to be rid of them. They would prefer to drive a lean, uncluttered vehicle, under tight control, steering straight toward well-marked goals. This is the difference between managers and leaders. We need leaders to govern the course of institutionalization. We need managers to deal with the practical problems of getting work done, counting costs, and ensuring accountability.

For managers, it is tempting to do whatever seems most efficient and effective in the near term; it seems rational to treat people and practices as properly subject to command and control. All seems justified by quick returns. From the standpoint of moral and social responsibility, however, managerial myopia is a distraction and a trap.

---

2. This sentence refashions the aphorism "Who says organization says oligarchy," by which Robert Michels summarized the thesis of his classic work *Political Parties: A Sociological Study of Oligarchical Tendencies in Modern Democracy* (1915; reprint, Glencoe, Ill.: Free Press, 1962).

Managerial myopia loses sight of the truth that people whose contributions are needed expect to be shown concern and respect. These demands are good for the enterprise. They improve communication, initiative, and morale. Therefore, no sharp line can be drawn between good management and moral obligation. Furthermore, a successful enterprise strives for good products, a special competence, good journalism, good education. To be successful, it must find ways of building those values into the structure of the organization and the attitudes of employees. Here again, moral obligations arise; here again, leaders must look beyond quick returns.

These ideas recall the writings of the "institutional" economists, who gave much attention to the large corporation.[3] *The Modern Corporation and Private Property* (1933), written by an economist, Gardiner C. Means, and a legal scholar, A. A. Berle, was a trenchant study of how the wide dispersion of stock ownership leads to self-perpetuating management. During the 1930s this analysis brought home the important changes taking place in modern business and raised questions about the meaning of property, the rights of shareholders, and the powers of corporate directors. These and other findings led some economists to conclude that the corporate enterprise should be understood "as an institution." In this view, the enterprise is a social reality, whose nature is determined by a specific historical, legal, and political setting; it is crucially dependent on many diverse interests for survival and success. Therefore, the enterprise is more than a legal entity and cannot be understood as an association of individual investors. Given this institutionalist theory, the foundations of enterprise responsibility are not far to seek. The freedom of management to do as it pleases is limited by forces it cannot wholly control. What was abstract becomes concrete, permeated by commitments and by the attendant obligations.

3. During the past century institutional economics has been a persistent counterpoint to mainstream economics. Thorstein Veblen, John R. Commons, and John Kenneth Galbraith, among others, insisted that economic activity should be seen as embedded in particular cultural and historical settings; subject to evolution, largely in response to new technologies; driven by contradictions, especially between the solid values of production and the destructive quest for riches; and crucially dependent on the good order and design of supportive institutions, such as the law of contracts, tax-supported services, and education. They thought the public interest must be protected from market failures by effective regulation and planning. A corollary is that economic institutions should not be treated as sacred or inevitable, at least in the forms they take at any given time.

RESPONSIBILITY FOR WHAT?

Probably no one would deny that corporations of all kinds must adhere to a baseline morality, or that this morality is properly enforced by law and government. Business pursues its legitimate ends while obeying many rules of right conduct, which forbid fraud, embezzlement, negligence, and much else. Like taxation, these are accepted costs of doing business. The enterprise lives within and not outside a moral order. Although organizations are not persons, they are *like* persons in that responsibility emerges from the experience of connectedness and the imperatives of interdependence.

The twentieth century saw a great expansion of public law enlarging the social responsibilities of business, especially in respect to labor relations; invidious discrimination based on race, gender, age, and disability; health and safety of employees and consumers; and environmental protection. These standards are *imposed* by the community. More difficult questions arise when we ask what responsibilities the enterprise should assume *voluntarily.* Whose interests should be served or protected by the corporate directors?

Like an individual person, the enterprise must take responsibility for its own existence, for its history and character, and for the impact of its activities on a variety of interests, both within and outside the organization. These responsibilities are not met by philanthropy. Obligations to avoid corruption, control pollution, and treat people fairly are more important, from the standpoint of corporate responsibility, than contributions to education, the arts, or even food banks for the poor.

The scope of responsibility depends in part on the enterprise's success. As we say of individuals, more is expected of the affluent than of those barely able to survive. Even the latter must obey the law and meet baseline standards of morality, but (as Aristotle pointed out long ago) it is the surplus that makes possible—and also enjoins—higher levels of moral responsibility.

This principle has special importance for the modern large corporation. A successful enterprise can readily attend to long-term effects, including the benefits of stability, cooperation, and trust. When its mission is defined as increasing "shareholder value *over time*,"[4]

---

4. "To increase shareholder value over time is the objective driving this enterprise" (Coca-Cola Company, annual report, 1984).

management can pursue strategies and make investments whose value may not be apparent. Furthermore, the successful large enterprise is often very rich and very powerful, capable of supporting collateral activities that benefit communities, including needy populations, without endangering the company's financial position.

Is there a corporate conscience? Yes, there is, or can be. A corporate conscience is created when values that transcend narrow self-interest are built into the practice and structure of the enterprise. This can be done in several ways: by clarifying policies and making them public; by practicing sensitive recruitment of staff; by inculcating appropriate attitudes and habits; by establishing special units to implement policies affecting the well-being of employees, or environmental and consumer protection; and by cooperating with relevant outside groups, such as trade unions and public agencies. All this becomes an "organizational culture," a framework within which the main goals of the enterprise are pursued. Although self-interest is by no means rejected, the realities of interdependence are accepted, the benefits of belonging acknowledged. Self-interest is moderated and redirected, not forgotten or extinguished.[5]

REINVENTING REGULATION

A corporate conscience may emerge in autonomous ways. But it is more likely to develop—and be fortified—by appropriate forms of regulation. Notable examples are the ways in which labor and environmental protection laws have affected business policies and organization. Three principles should govern:

First, the activities to be regulated are, for the most part, desirable as well as troubling. There is usually no question of shutting down production of chemicals, steel, or automobiles; no desire to stamp out the work of hospitals or railroads. Rather, we want regulation to sustain and encourage productive work while protecting the community from what economists call "negative externalities"— that is, from unwanted effects such as poor air and water quality,

---

5. As I noted in chapter 3, self-interest includes self-esteem, which depends to a large extent on feelings of rightness and self-justification. What we think of ourselves reflects the views of others. Hence, self-regard is an important spur to moral responsibility, among organizations as well as individual persons.

preventable accidents, or oppressive working conditions. The need to protect and improve as well as control is a necessary premise of sound regulatory policy.

Second, smart regulation is sensitive to variation—that is, to important differences among industries and firms with respect to how they are organized, the technologies they use, and the special dangers they pose. Taking account of differences makes regulation more effective and less heavy-handed.

Third, a spirit of cooperation and problem solving should prevail. Effective regulation demands intimate knowledge of operations, including what options are practical and least costly, what incentives for workers and managers will improve safety or quality control, what new technologies will abate pollution, how to monitor and report unwanted effects. The idea is to encourage joint problem solving rather than mindless obedience (or systematic evasion) and to do so without losing sight of the public interest. Cooperative regulation transforms "targets" into "clients." The clients need respect and understanding, but they also need help, guidance, and authority. Without effective authority, cooperation is degraded, and public agencies may be "captured" by more powerful business interests.

The aim is *maximum feasible self-regulation.* This principle recalls a distinction drawn above, in chapter 3, between accountability and responsibility. Accountability imposes an external standard. Responsibility internalizes standards by building them into the self-conceptions, motivations, and habits of individuals and into the organization's premises and routines. As in so much of social life, we try to get people to want to do what they should do.

Self-regulation is desirable because it is likely to be more effective than external control, and because it preserves and strengthens the self-sustaining institutions of civil society. This strategy has been called "responsive" regulation.[6]

Individual firms within a competitive environment cannot be relied on, by themselves, to be responsible and self-restrained.[7] One

6. Ian Ayres and John Braithwaite, *Responsive Regulation* (New York: Oxford University Press, 1992).

7. For new thinking on regulation, see Ayres and Braithwaite, *Responsive Regulation;* Eugene Bardach and Robert Kagan, *Going by the Book* (Philadelphia: Temple University Press, 1982); Eugene Bardach, *Getting Agencies to Work Together* (Washington, D.C.: Brookings Institution Press, 1998); Neil Gunningham and Peter Grabosky, *Smart Regulation* (Oxford: Clarendon Press, 1998).

strategy focuses on *industries* rather than on individual companies, as Joseph Rees did in his research on the American nuclear power and chemical industries.[8] Rees found that effective industry-based institutions could be created for enforcing safety standards. These cases are selective in that they involve industries haunted by catastrophe. The nuclear power industry was energized by the 1979 disaster at Three Mile Island; the chemical industry, by the 1984 calamity in Bhopal, India. Still, under modern conditions of mass marketing—standardized pharmaceuticals, hamburgers, soft drinks, and automobiles—public safety is not a small or exceptional concern. Industry-wide standards, largely self-enforced, should be well-established features of production and marketing.

Responsive or cooperative regulation is facilitative, problem-centered, and minimally intrusive. It is an example of what I referred to earlier as shared governance. The aim is *better* regulation by government, drawing on richer, more effective resources, not deregulation. In this context, shared governance knits public and private goals and resources. A large business, a health maintenance organization, a university: all have rules and policies, serving their own purposes in the light of their own needs. Properly designed, these internal systems of law and morality can serve the public good as well. In the communitarian vision, a blurring of boundaries makes sense.[9]

A preference for self-regulation does not preclude a prominent role for government. We cannot do without the authority to establish baseline standards prohibiting negligence, or institutional racism, or disregard for harms done to individuals, or to public goods, such as clean air and water. We must often look to government to get self-regulation started, as was done in the collective-bargaining legislation of the 1930s. An ideal of self-regulation should guide and inform the work of government; it does not eliminate the need for social learning and collective judgment, or for government agencies whose task is to define and defend the public interest.

---

8. Joseph Rees, *Hostages of Each Other* (Chicago: University of Chicago Press, 1994); Rees, "Development of Communitarian Regulation in the Chemical Industries," *Law and Policy* 19 (October 1997): 477–528.

9. In contrast, the liberal tradition has favored walls of separation between social spheres: law and morality, law and politics, public and private, economy and society.

THE PEOPLE'S BUSINESS

Even the most ardent advocates of competitive capitalism and the profit motive acknowledge the reality of "market failure." Economists have no difficulty recognizing that market mechanisms will often fail to protect the public interest. Of course, the general welfare will be served in *some* important ways, if people diligently seek their own benefit. Goods and services will be produced and marketed; competition will improve quality and lessen cost. Nevertheless, a benign outcome is not assured. The common good is often sacrificed to short-term economic gains; people may not get the information they need regarding the safety or quality of products; convenient alternatives may not be provided; consumers may be vulnerable to psychic distractions or unhealthy temptations. To offset these dangers, the free play of markets is subject to many rules, such as those governing the quality of food and medicine, pollution, land use, construction of roads and sewers, education, police protection, and much else that calls for political decision and government intervention. Although market solutions to some of these problems may be appropriate, creating financial incentives to encourage better practices and new technologies, we cannot rely on those measures to fully protect public health and safety, or to promote the arts, education, and science. There is nothing surprising or radical about this conclusion.

An especially insidious market failure occurs when a product or service that directly affects the quality of public life is degraded, killed, or unborn.[10] An important contemporary example is the media industry, which includes television news and news-related programs, the Internet, book and magazine publishing, and major art exhibits. In these activities we see an increasing conflict between what Thorstein Veblen called "the pecuniary interest" and standards of quality or "workmanship."[11] As pressure rises for wider markets and higher profits, precarious values are displaced or eroded. To maximize sales, textbooks are "dumbed down" by making their contents as bland, accessible, and inoffensive as possible. As television news

10. Of course, many other businesses are "affected with a public interest": for instance, banking, pharmaceuticals, logging. Each places a significant value at risk; each requires a customized strategy for dealing with market failures.

11. Thorstein Veblen, *The Instinct of Workmanship* (1914; reprint, New York: W. W. Norton, 1964).

programs, especially at local stations, become important "profit centers," a "race to the bottom" occurs. News as entertainment emphasizes human-interest stories and crime reports, which can be presented vividly, cheaply, and quickly. Print journalism is a vast sea of mediocrity, punctuated by islands of quality and professionalism. Before the last half of the twentieth century, much of the media industry was marked by low or modest profitability. Publishers often combined commercial necessity with vocational commitment. In the book trade, for example, it was long taken for granted that profits would be limited and that editors would be drawn from a world of book lovers and devotees of literature, not from among marketing specialists indifferent to content or quality.[12] Furthermore, literary, educational, and journalistic ideals were sustained by a professional sensibility. Small independent firms could develop distinctive identities and could decide for themselves what level of profitability would be tolerable. The merging of publishing firms, television stations, motion picture studios, and newspapers into large corporate conglomerates has created a very different commercial environment. In a world that strives for maximum profit and shareholder returns, a "cash cow" is something everyone wants—and needs. This temptation is at war with the ethos of a creative enterprise.

The most notable exceptions, in newspaper publishing, have relied on a sometimes vigorous hybrid: the family enterprise. The large family business is an anachronism today, long since turned over to professional managers in whom Wall Street can have confidence. Exceptions are a few family dynasties committed to upholding the quality of journalism while maintaining prudent but not maximum levels of profitability. This strategy required (and made possible) a wall of separation between the business side of the enterprise (finance, marketing, advertising) and the work of reporting, writing, and editing. Protecting the integrity of editing and reporting was taken to be a prime institutional necessity.[13]

We can draw an important lesson from this experience. Society needs new ways of doing what was previously done by limited-profit firms and family trusts. We need to do by public policy and

12. Jason Epstein, "The Rattle of Pebbles," *New York Review of Books,* April 27, 2000, p. 55.
13. Regarding the history of the *New York Times,* see Susan Tifft and Alex Jones, *The Trust* (Boston: Little, Brown, 1999).

institutional design what was earlier done less consciously, or sustained by family pride or by the psychic rewards of a modestly successful business based on a vocation or craft. One promising option would expand the role of "not-for-profit" enterprises.[14] This independent sector (which was discussed earlier, in chapter 5) can help rescue many market casualties.[15] Not-for-profit enterprises are currently providing low-income housing, medical care, and public radio and television programming. Some are supported by religious communities; many depend on the help of volunteers. In this work moral idealism is combined with economic realism. Resources must be mobilized, investments monitored, costs controlled. These activities are not untouched by market forces. But the so-called "nonprofits" can resist the market's indifference to culture and morality. If social policy encourages these associations and activities, it will acknowledge the worth and redeem the promise of civil society.

14. We might also require compensation from those who seriously endanger the quality of culture and public discourse, such as a tax imposed on the telecommunications industry to support educational and public-service programming *in addition to* its own responsibilities for serving those needs.

15. Benjamin Gidron, Ralph M. Kramer, and Lester M. Salamon, eds., *Government and the Third Sector* (San Francisco: Jossey-Bass, 1992). Also Robert Wuthnow, *Between States and Markets: The Voluntary Sector in Comparative Perspective* (Princeton, N.J.: Princeton University Press, 1991).

CHAPTER 9

SOCIAL JUSTICE

Among the ideals we associate with community, none is more important, none more controversial, than the quest for justice. Justice is a communitarian imperative. Communities need relief from the abuse of power and private violence; justice brings peace by settling disputes and determining rights. Furthermore, as we saw in chapter 2, the experience of community includes self-interest and conflict as well as solidarity. Justice speaks to these urgencies. It does so in the name of the community, in accents of civility, with the rod of authority.

Justice strengthens community by fixing and clarifying principles of good order, including rights of property, kinship, and citizenship. These shared understandings underpin the arrangements and transactions of everyday life. Some principles of justice, based on human nature and the necessities of social life, lead to universally recognized rules—for example, against murder, or in support of the authority of parents. Other principles are time-bound products of the special history of a particular community. Although principles of justice are often contested, many are unquestioned, experienced as part of a stable and secure world.

WHY "SOCIAL" JUSTICE?

The everyday work of a system of justice deals with individual cases: this plaintiff or defendant in an accident case; this person arrested by the police or on trial for a crime; this employee or student accused of misconduct; this relative seeking custody of a child. In these cases, rules and procedures are taken as given. In contrast, *social* justice shifts attention from individual circumstances and settled rules to a broader assessment of how justice is done, not only by government but in the community as a whole. To test the quality of justice, rules, procedures, and the outcomes they produce are subject to criticism and open to reconstruction. This criticism brings to bear our best understanding of what justice means and what it requires.

Hayek's Mistake. A prominent economist and social philosopher, Friedrich A. Hayek, called social justice a "mirage."[1] In support of this conclusion Hayek relied on a distinction between *responsible actors* (organizations or persons) and *spontaneous orders.* The former make conscious choices, for which they may be held responsible. "Spontaneous orders" are unplanned outcomes of many individual decisions. According to Hayek, what individual persons or organizations do may be considered just or unjust, but it makes no sense, he wrote, to demand responsibility from a market or a social condition, which does not "act" and which no one designs or controls. If demands for justice are to be meaningful, they must be addressed to responsible actors—that is, to people and groups able to make choices, control events, and produce results. Furthermore, said Hayek, to get a particular outcome from a spontaneous order, we would have to subject society to an all-powerful government. Therefore, because it cares about outcomes, social justice is bound to be an idle dream or, in Hayek's view, despotic socialism. The mirage would be a nightmare.

This argument is mistaken because it misunderstands or ignores a central idea—the concept of a "social system." Social systems (which give shape to particular organizations as well as "society") are patterned ways of relating and thinking, typically based on how power, dependency, wealth, and opportunity are distributed and ex-

---

1. *The Mirage of Social Justice,* vol. 2 of *Law, Legislation and Liberty* (London: Routledge, 1976). Much admired by contemporary American conservatives, Hayek thought of himself as a liberal, proclaiming the virtues of autonomy and the dangers of socialism.

perienced. When we study these realities, we can ask: Are the patterns justified? Are the rules fair? What kinds of self-interest are encouraged, discouraged, or tempered by concern for the common good?
Is there convincing evidence of hostile discrimination, exploitation,
or blocked opportunity? These conditions may be found in a business or other special-purpose organization, perhaps in the form of
institutional racism. They may well be unplanned outcomes of employment, education or residence.[2]

In appraising a social system, it does not really matter that it
emerges from many individual decisions. Such decisions are usually
made within an accepted framework of rules and premises—for example, rules affecting the inheritance of property or benefits given to
some people and not others. The resulting pattern may be oppressive
and unjust. For African Americans, it would be a travesty to say that
the "state of affairs" that creates racial discrimination is bad but not
unjust.

The meaning of social justice cannot be found in a single criterion, such as the fair distribution of resources. Social justice seeks
remedies for all the ways in which people are oppressed, including
overly intrusive policing and the unchecked power of private groups.
Social justice is also sensitive to the needs of future generations.
What Hayek failed to understand is that injustice may stem from
established patterns of social organization, regardless of individual
intent or accountability.

He also missed the point that the quest for social justice is
mainly about relief from oppression, not the achievement of an ideal
or perfect society. Social justice puts us on the road to a good society, but its special mission is more limited. A good society encourages prosperity, supports excellence in the arts and sciences, and
strives for nobility as well as decency, compassion as well as responsibility, fraternity as well as self-restraint. In contrast, social
justice, like all justice, is mainly concerned with fairness, respect,
and freedom from oppression. This does not mean it is untouched by
higher ideals. Justice entails fidelity to truth, respect for persons,
awareness of the evils that come from stunted lives and betrayed
hopes.

2. Thus we speak of de facto segregation even when legal or de jure segregation is
absent.

THE RULE OF LAW

Social justice begins with the rule of law. Every community needs something like a legal framework to regulate the forms and govern the expectations of social life. The rudiments (at least) of a legal order are found in every human community: some way of fixing the rights and responsibilities arising from kinship, maturity, and economic life; some way of deciding which duties will be enforced, which claims of right will be honored. Law is an indispensable agency of community, and the nature of the legal order tells us much about the character of the community. At one extreme law may be highly repressive, regulating conduct in all spheres of life and in great detail. Some religious communities are organized in this way, and the totalitarian regimes of Nazism and communism were ugly examples of oppressive law. In more ordinary communities, however, the autonomy of persons and groups is more likely to be respected. Although many choices are regulated, they are not necessarily rigidly controlled or prescribed.

The "rule of law" is *law plus standards*—that is, law subject to criticism by (and inviting appeals to) rules and principles governing how laws are made, applied, and obeyed. These standards keep law within bounds. They limit those who would abuse power under color of law. A primary function of the rule of law is to restrain the power of kings, presidents, and other executive officials. A "government of laws and not of men" is proclaimed: no official, however mighty, is above the law. More broadly understood, the rule of law restrains judges and legislators as well as executives and agencies. A written or unwritten constitution provides standards for testing official acts of all kinds, bringing to bear a "law behind the law," which says when authority is exceeded or when rights are abridged.

In a community governed by the rule of law, the fundamental autonomy of individuals and groups is protected. The assumption is that people should, for the most part, make their own choices and conduct their own affairs. The government uses law to protect the necessary conditions of collective life, such as public safety, and to create a framework within which the pursuit of private ends will be compatible with the public interest, including the public interest in fulfilled obligations. The free markets of capitalism can be neither free nor effective without rules ensuring orderly business and the stability of expectations.

In its broadest significance the rule of law sustains a culture of lawfulness. Where the rule of law prevails, most people honor "justice under law," most accept a prima facie obligation of respect and obedience.

Much depends on the law's capacity to deliver more than formal justice. In formal justice legal proprieties are recognized; judges are honest and independent; rules of evidence are respected; statutes are properly enacted. What may be missing, however, is a genuine concern for just outcomes, affected by all the ways in which the process may go wrong, perhaps distorted by overzealous prosecution or by a pattern of disadvantage to which the system is blind. The quest for social justice seeks a more sensitive, more responsive legal order. This richer conception of the rule of law strengthens the connection between law and justice, and between law and community as well.

MORAL EQUALITY

Ideally, under the rule of law, justice is blind to special privilege; like cases are dealt with in like ways. This *legal* equality is driven by a deeper concern for *moral* equality. People differ widely in the talents they have and the efforts they make. These and other differences lead to many inequalities, which we accept and even foster despite our commitment to moral equality. To be "dedicated to the proposition that all men are created equal," as President Lincoln put it at Gettysburg, is to say that every human person is equally deserving of respect and concern.

However, the realities of social life always limit the egalitarian ideal. The challenge is to maintain and advance the ideal, while accepting differences that benefit the community as a whole.

This challenge has played a lively role in U.S. constitutional history. The Fourteenth Amendment, adopted in the wake of the Civil War, guaranteed to all persons (not just citizens) "the equal protection of the laws." In the late nineteenth century and the early decades of the twentieth, the Supreme Court gave this principle a narrow reading. Looking to form rather than substance, the justices shrank from close scrutiny of laws that vindicated prejudice and perpetuated subordination.[3] In time, however, as social and biological science

---

3. For example, the Supreme Court allowed laws banning miscegenation and upholding racial segregation.

advanced, and as the moral awareness of the community was raised, the meaning of legal equality was greatly expanded. The Court broadened that principle to take account of the damage suffered by victims of oppression or exclusion, especially African Americans and other historically disadvantaged minorities. In the new era, the Equal Protection Clause would be understood as a promise to protect the fundamental rights of all persons and all citizens. The constitutional mandate would thereby become a mainstay of inclusion and therefore of community.

Although moral equality does not require social equality, the two are connected in important ways. Social inequalities breed contempt, especially when those who have least must live under degrading and dehumanizing conditions. Moral equality is hard to sustain when some people are endowed with privilege and honor, while others are thought of as a lesser breed, brutish, untalented, untrustworthy, and undeserving.

Moral equality is the keystone in the arch of social justice. The idea that "all men are created equal" envisions a society that cares for all its members. Social justice is not social equality. It is, however, a standpoint from which we assess inequalities and question exclusions.

EFFECTIVE OPPORTUNITY

In the liberal tradition there is a sovereign remedy for the wounds inflicted on moral equality by systems of privilege and attitudes of contempt—equality of opportunity. Since the seventeenth century the chief target of liberal criticism has been the caste principle. In a new era of enlarged opportunity, merit and competence would prevail, and privilege would be dethroned. In government patronage and precedence would be eliminated. Ordinary people would be able to live, work, marry, study, vote, and hold office, according to their interests, inclinations, and abilities, unvexed by the restrictions of class, race, or religion. In the nineteenth century this agenda was enlarged to include opposition to slavery, racial oppression, and the subordination of women. These efforts continued through the twentieth century. *Legal* oppression and exclusion remained the chief concerns. This is understandable because in the movements for abolition of slavery and for women's rights, the first objective had to be equality before the law.

These efforts have been haunted by the unforgiving ghost of justice denied—in fact as well as form, in life as well as law. As I noted in chapter 1, liberal strategies have long sought *substantive* justice and *effective* freedom. This quest set the stage for what became, in the late twentieth century, a divisive conflict. Liberal spokesmen focused on the essentials of citizenship and personhood, such as the right to vote without coercion, unrestricted by property qualifications, or to be free of exclusions and impediments based on race, sex, or religion. These reforms did not necessarily bring down the social barriers to opportunity, nor could they, by themselves, remedy the effects of past injustice. They did not ensure equality of opportunity in the work force, in education, or in political life. Although liberals had high hopes that these good things would come to pass, a major stumbling block was the very argument they made on behalf of civil rights. The ideas they deployed in opposing prejudice could be used to justify policies that blocked effective equality of opportunity.

This irony was starkly revealed in the controversy over "affirmative action" during the last decades of the twentieth century. Affirmative action sought to make opportunity effective by reaching out to disadvantaged groups in ways that would improve their chances for employment and education. The strategies ranged from relatively uncontroversial efforts to increase the pool of qualified applicants to highly controversial polices calling for "targets" and "quotas." To meet such goals, or show a good-faith effort to do so, the programs gave preference (of various sorts and degrees) to applicants from disadvantaged groups. Two liberal premises were at risk: (1) the idea that institutional policy should be color-blind; and (2) the idea that, in a regime of equal opportunity, occupational or educational merit should be the only legitimate criterion for hiring, admission, or advancement.

The imagery of color-blindness had great appeal. In a famous dissent from the majority opinion in *Plessy v. Ferguson* (1896), Justice John Marshall Harlan wrote: "the Constitution of the United States does not, I think, permit any public authority to know the race of those entitled to be protected. . . . Our Constitution is color-blind." But Justice Harlan also said: "What can more certainly arouse race hate, what can more certainly create and perpetuate a feeling of distrust between these races, than state enactments which, in fact,

proceed on the ground that colored citizens are so inferior and degraded that they cannot be allowed to sit in public coaches occupied
by white citizens? That, as all will admit, is the real meaning of such
legislation as was enacted in Louisiana."[4] Harlan made "color-blind"
a liberal motto. But this obscured the real insight in his dissent.

The issue was not race as such, but the treatment of race as a
badge of inferiority and a justification for oppression. The problem
was not "discrimination," which is necessary for any classification,
but *invidious* discrimination, which defines a class of people as ob-
noxious or unworthy. Noninvidious classification is easily justified
and often necessary. For many good purposes we distinguish farmers
from other producers, affluent from poorer taxpayers, children from
adults, boys from girls. These classifications may bring special benefits, or impose special burdens, but they are not necessarily invidious. They are always debatable, and sometimes suspect, as in the case
of some distinctions between men and women. In the fight against
affirmative action, political rhetoric has obscured the distinction
between invidious and noninvidious classifications. Giving special
opportunities to African Americans may be costly to some white
Americans, and the policy may properly be questioned on other
grounds, but not because those who lose out are considered inherently less worthy or less deserving than others.

When the Civil Rights laws were passed by Congress in the 1960s,
it was implicitly understood that the evil to be fought was treating
African Americans and women as inherently inferior. This understanding underlay the Supreme Court's rejection of the "separate but
equal" doctrine. Racism and sexism were to be corrected by rejecting
classifications intended to condone or perpetuate invidious discrimination, or having the effect of doing so. This strategy did not bar
legitimate classifications based on the many ways in which people
differ, or are differently situated.

To vindicate the moral equality of African Americans, women,
and other minorities, American lawmakers could not be blind to
prejudice and stigma. Moreover, even very weak forms of affirmative
action, intended to bring minorities within the pool of qualified
candidates, while avoiding preferences in hiring or admissions, could

4. 163 U.S. 537, 554, 559, 560 (1896).

not be implemented without "knowing the race" or ethnicity of the affected populations.

Communitarians support affirmative action because division based on moral stigma destroys community; and because every member of the community is entitled to full and untainted membership. Effective equality of opportunity advances social unity. It does so by protecting the right of every person to share the rewards and responsibilities of belonging, including the benefits of prosperity and the burdens of service. Therefore, the proper goal of affirmative action is unity, not diversity. Diversity can enrich the experience of community by broadening the horizons of neighbors, employees, and students. But in affirmative action the aim is full citizenship; the guiding star is our common humanity.

An ideal of moral equality encourages people to see each other as fellow students, employees, professionals, citizens. This fellow-feeling is sustained by attitudes that prize justice and welcome strangers. To create that moral climate, the realities of ordinary life must be confronted, not ignored. A realistic conception of effective opportunity is needed. In addition to removing barriers, we may need to do positive things. In education, for example, we provide extra resources for poor children, to make up for inadequate support at home. Every community must face up to its own history, including how that history has crippled lives and limited chances. This cannot be done without using categories we may not like, such as sex, race, and ethnicity.

Although effective equality of opportunity is a fine ideal, it takes us only part of the way toward moral equality. Competition must be open, and rewards must be fair, but what happens to those who do not or cannot "make it"? If we care about every person, social justice must reach beyond meritocracy. Meritocracy makes sense in the right places, where skill and achievement are crucial. Yet we need other ways of recognizing everyone's equal worth, whatever their individual talents, ambitions, or handicaps, whatever their will to succeed or readiness to compete.

Looking beyond meritocracy means, for example, assuming that every child can learn. This doctrine does not preclude rewards for excellence. The prizes go to the best and brightest, who are well rewarded in school, and in life after leaving school. But the commitment to every child has nothing to do with competition or prizes. As a principle of responsible education it is a legitimate and compelling challenge to the design, staffing, and leadership of schools and colleges. We need not and should not abandon meritocracy. We should give it a proper place within a community committed to social justice.

JUSTICE AND STEWARDSHIP

Doing justice presumes an ethic of responsibility: we cannot act justly without safeguarding the interests—patients, clients, children, institutions—we have bound ourselves to defend. This is the fidelity we call stewardship, which is responsible concern for a particular relationship, group, practice, or resource. In the Judeo-Christian idiom, people in authority are God's delegates and trustees. They are stewards of His dominion. In this way power is limited by moral ideals, so that interests subject to the steward's control are protected and nurtured. The most important form of stewardship is the duty we owe to future generations. This is a burden we accept along with the benefits of belonging.

Thomas Jefferson famously declared that "the earth belongs to the living and not to the dead."[5] There is much to be said for a public philosophy that makes each generation its own master. But Jefferson's "declaration of generational independence"[6] is hardly a communitarian idea. More congenial are the words of Edmund Burke, who thought of society as "a partnership, not only between those who are living, but between those who are living, those who are dead, and those who are to be born."[7] Responsibility runs to what we have taken from the past as well as to the ways in which we shape our children's future.

Justice as stewardship is implicit in the conception of corporate

5. Thomas Jefferson to James Madison, written from Paris, September 6, 1789, in *The Life and Selected Writings of Thomas Jefferson*, edited by A. Akochand and W. Peden (New York: Random House, 1944), p. 492. In this letter, Jefferson was mainly concerned with lifting the dead hand of the past, not with responsibility for future generations. Indeed, he emphasized that each generation should pay its own debts, without burdening future generations. He also said, at another point, that "the earth *in its usufruct* belongs to the living" (emphasis added).

6. As Edmund S. Morgan called it, *New York Review of Books*, July 20, 2000, p. 47.

7. *Reflections on the Revolution in France* (1790; reprint, New York: Liberal Arts Press, 1955), p. 110.

responsibility I sketched in chapter 8. Another example, more self-conscious and insistent, is the movement for environmental protection. Environmentalists have fought hard to substitute an ideal of stewardship for the unregulated exploitation of nature. They have helped create a moral bond between humanity and nature. This bond is the basis of stewardship, which, in serving the interests of future generations, is an authentic expression of social justice.

ROADS TO INCLUSION

Equal opportunity and an ethic of stewardship take us part of the way toward a just community. But social justice is offended by every kind of stigma and prejudice, every barrier to respect and inclusion. The greatest wounds to the human spirit come from racial, religious, and ethnic enmities. Although affirmations of identity have many benefits, they are all too often associated with hatred, pride, and contempt. To combat these evils, we must sometimes make hard choices. It may be necessary, for example, to "know the race" of African Americans, despite a well-founded reluctance to enshrine in law such a morally tainted and scientifically offensive category as "race." Yet we may have to do so in order to make opportunity effective and law realistic. Similarly, "hate crime" is a troublesome but justified invention. Although we prefer to punish deeds, not thoughts or attitudes, we cannot turn a blind eye to the social reality of acts inspired by abominable thoughts. In hate crimes the punishment is not for thoughts alone, but for acts made especially blameworthy by the hatred and intolerance they express.[8]

Inclusion and Difference. The quest for justice does not preclude—on the contrary it demands—respect for particular identities, diverse histories, and special obligations. To be inclusive, we must take seriously how people live and the circumstances they face. Disabled persons cannot be full participants in the life of the community if they are not able to work and learn and get about. The community must recognize their special needs and potential contributions. Inclusion of religious, political, and ethnic minorities is meaningless if it does not respect their special histories and traditions.

8. Beatings and other harmful acts, of course, would be crimes regardless of the special motivation, but the latter adds a strong reason for deterrence and punishment.

In an interview conducted during the 2000 presidential campaign, Vice President Al Gore defended his support for affirmative action by stressing the interdependence of inclusion and difference. Speaking of race relations in America, Gore perceived a "two-step process":

> You have to first establish absolute and genuine mutual respect for difference. And that respect for difference has to include both an appreciation for the unique suffering that has come about because of the difference, and the unique gifts and contributions that have come about because of the difference. And a basic appreciation for the unique perspective that is based on the difference. Then the second step is a transcendence of that difference to embrace all the elements that we have in common in the human spirit.[9]

This analysis recognizes what I referred to earlier as the irrepressible tension between outward-looking and inward-looking aspects of community. Parochial passions must yield to the just but limited claims of larger unities, including our common humanity. At the same time, the benefits of particularity—kinship, locality, ethnicity, religion, occupation—are granted importance, even at some cost to more universal ideals. A balance must be struck in the light of the context at hand. In caring for young children, we give great weight to the special obligations of parents; citizenship calls for more impersonal judgments and a different kind of loyalty.

Curbing Inequality. In a normal community many forms of inequality must be accepted. We need not shrink from that conclusion. Effective government, sound education, economic prosperity, a rich culture—for these we need investors, leaders, managers, professionals, creative artists. To gain their best efforts, we offer them special privileges and rewards. Therefore, we cannot and should not try to eliminate inequality. However, *gross* inequalities are another matter, because they weaken solidarity and erode respect. Gross inequalities divide haves and have-nots into different social worlds. The rich and powerful set themselves apart from populations they fear and for whom they have contempt. At risk is the experience of common membership, a sense of common fate, and a cooperative search for

9. Nicholas Lemann, "Gore without a Script," *New Yorker,* July 31, 2000, p. 62.

the common good. Furthermore, democracy is corrupted by the intimacies of wealth and power. The communitarian alternative is a society unmarred by wide disparities of wealth and income, with no great gulf between the contributions people make and the compensations they get, and informed by the truth that an individual's good fortune owes much to a community's resources and institutions. From those to whom much is given, we properly ask more open pockets and an extra measure of civic virtue.

Curbing inequality is not an egalitarian project. It is not driven by an abstract ideal of equality or by a desire for social leveling. Nor does it disparage elites. Leaders and activists of many kinds, in many spheres of life—artists, writers, judges, ministers, scholars, athletes, entrepreneurs, politicians, organizers, professionals of all sorts—give life to values and make them secure.

Remaking the Safety Net. Uncurbed inequality offers the grim prospect of an underclass, for whom poverty is absolute, not relative deprivation. The point is not that some people suffer because they have fewer goods and comforts than others. Their condition is more serious. When people are ill fed, ill housed, ill educated, excluded from opportunity, wanting in self-respect, they cannot participate in the life-sustaining worlds of family and work, or they do so inadequately and in distorted ways. To treat the poor justly and to avoid the great costs of exclusion, we need not demand social equality. What matters is the assurance of a decent human life: adequate food and health, good education, good jobs. The great problem for social policy is how to provide these necessities without impairing self-reliance or discouraging self-improvement. A prudent conception of the safety net would reject the idea of a guaranteed minimum income, insofar as such an entitlement divorces benefits from obligations. Instead we look for better ways of encouraging responsible participation in community life: work rather than welfare, job training, job creation. The premise is that a good job—a living wage and good conditions—is the best path to inclusion, the mainstay of self-respect, a pillar of social justice.

Understood in this way, the safety net upholds an ethic of responsibility. A community shows *collective* responsibility when it provides the resources and opportunities people need for *personal* responsibility. This public philosophy has confidence in the moral character of people made whole by supportive and nurturing communities.

PART THREE

HORIZONS

THE COMMON GOOD

A COMMON FAITH

CHAPTER 10

THE COMMON GOOD

LIBERAL DOUBTS AND FEARS

In modern thought, especially liberal thought, "the common good" is greeted with at most two cheers. The most important source of this skepticism is a perceived threat to liberty. Defenders of liberty like to think of the interests we have and the judgments we make as properly individual rather than collective. Only individual persons and particular groups have genuine interests and ideals. Liberty is at risk when we suppose that officials or legislators, speaking for the community, can say what is good for all. Individuals are the best judges of their own interests. They do not need Big Brother to tell them how to live or what choices to make. In this view, the community should limit itself to setting the rules within which private judgments can be made and private interests pursued. Such interests are definite, solid, and readily determined by expressions of preference. The public interest is much harder to define and may well be a screen behind which power calls the tune and injustice is protected.

This argument does add a note of realism to our understanding of public life. It encourages personal responsibility in making choices, good or bad. It respects the judgments of individual persons, who are, as we saw in chapter 4, the most important and irreducible components of what I called the "unity of unities."

These ideas are important contributions to the public philosophy

of a free people. But they make the common good even more uncertain and difficult to grasp than it has to be. This uncertainty gives
license to ignore, or be indifferent to, what we owe to others and the
needs we share.

The common good is also undermined by the widespread acceptance of moral skepticism and relativism. These doctrines have
been embraced by a great many supporters of "popular" liberalism,
if only because they are handy arguments against the claim that a
particular status quo is the voice of reason or the only option we have.
Relativists can justify disdain for conventional morality by denying
that it has a foundation in truth. They can go further and say that all
claims to authority are unfounded and self-serving.

Beyond popular liberalism, in the more subtle realm of political
theory, a more careful and coherent argument is offered. Here the
common good is not disparaged as pointless, mystical, or an idle
dream, but is viewed as a virtue of procedure rather than substance,
of means rather than ends. According to this understanding, if the political process is fair and protects fundamental rights, the outcome
will be a satisfactory expression of the common good.

This strategy calls for political self-restraint. The fundamental law
of a liberal community—a written or unwritten constitution—will
not try to say what is a good society, a good person, or even a good citizen. Instead, the constitution will leave such judgments to individuals, families, churches, and other associations, so long as they do not
try to impose their convictions on others. The great value to be preserved is freedom of conscience; the great means to that end is toleration; the great outcome is social unity. Therefore, we should not say
too much about the common good. A regime of reticence is prescribed.

This reticent or "neutralist" liberalism does not flow from an abstract or speculative theory of what freedom requires. It derives from
some hard lessons of history, especially the long train of shameful
abuses imposed on humanity by religious, ethnic, and ideological enmities. The lesson to be drawn is that politics should not be about
salvation or perfection. Deep differences are inevitable, and very
dangerous. Therefore, we should not seek consensus on personal or
social ideals. Better to live in peace by agreeing to disagree about how
our lives should be lived or what is the best society.[1]

1. See John Rawls, *Political Liberalism* (New York: Columbia University Press, 1993).

Religious and quasi-religious conflicts have certainly led to great evils, and this truth underpins the constitutional principles of the First Amendment: separation of church and state (no "establishment of religion"); protection of the "free exercise" of religion and of "the freedom of speech." The American public philosophy is to this extent neutralist, to this extent reticent.

Does this background require us to adopt a more wide-ranging principle of neutrality? Does it warrant a retreat from collective judgments about bigotry, education, inequality, peace, abortion, and euthanasia? Should we deny to democratic government the authority to decide what is good for personal and social well-being?

The liberal mind has fixed its attention on the many devils that divide us and the myriad flowers that bloom. Autonomy, plurality, conflict, disagreement: these are the prime realities of social life, the great concerns of politics, the foundations of institutional design. A premise is that differences run deep; they are chasms precariously bridged by narrow planks.

The communitarian alternative has a surer grasp on the realities of coherence and the need for consensus. Reflection and dialogue address the goodness of our lives, not only the more limited objective of keeping a society from falling apart. The appeal is to substance as well as procedure. Instead of treating the common good as fraught with danger and at best elusive, we look to the promise of collective intelligence. What makes for the common good is necessarily open to inquiry and subject to debate. Nevertheless, communitarians, pragmatists, and other "new liberals" have this (and more) in common: confidence in social learning and in the capacity of a well-formed community to meet new problems and take advantage of new opportunities for improving the lives of individual persons and their communities.

At stake is a substantive or "thick" conception of the common good. No serious thinker has been wholly indifferent to the general welfare as a criterion for judging public philosophies and policies. But the common good can be a thin and anemic idea, especially when a political or economic doctrine questions the reality and the moral worth of cooperation, interdependence, and consensus. The integrity of institutions and the quality of public life seem less real if they can be readily "deconstructed," that is, reduced to the choices and motives of individuals—the true centers of energy and creativity. The interests of the community are made to seem remote, intangible, and of lesser worth.[2]

VARIETIES OF CONSENSUS

Much has been written by liberal theorists about the limits of consensus and the prevalence of disagreement.[3] To make sense of this argument, we should know what consensus means and what the quest for it entails. A first step is to recognize that there are different kinds of consensus. We should distinguish *constitutional* consensus from *policy* (or legislative) consensus. Our Constitution surely contemplates lively controversy, and most questions of policy are left for future consideration by the people and their lawmaking representatives. Framed "for the ages," the U.S. Constitution deals only with the powers and structure of government and with basic principles, such as freedom of speech and association. The Constitution presumes agreement on these matters. However, much room is left for different conceptions of spiritual salvation and moral rightness, and for different understandings of how to draw the line between public and private interests or whether political institutions should be based on pessimism or optimism. The Constitution is spacious, but it is the product of agreement on foundational ideas, which become more compelling as they gain the reverence of the people and the authority of history. These shared understandings include ways of interpreting necessarily general clauses, such as those dealing with "commerce," "the freedom of speech," "equal protection of the laws," or "cruel and unusual punishment." As U.S. history has shown, constitutional interpretation is no stranger to consensus—its formation and reconstruction, its trials and ordeals.[4]

Policy consensus is closer to everyday political life. It is the great

2. This outlook finds support in postmodern theories of culture and society, whose main message is one of pervasive incoherence.

3. A recent example is John Gray, *Two Faces of Liberalism* (New York: New Press, 2000).

4. The Supreme Court made major contributions to political consensus when it expanded the meaning of "freedom of speech" to include artistic as well as political expression, and when it rejected the doctrine of "separate but equal," which it had accepted in the nineteenth century. It is not always so successful, as the continuing controversy regarding the Court's 1973 decision in *Roe v. Wade* shows.

prize sought in deploying arguments and building coalitions. Although many proposals have only shallow support and become law only by virtue of slim majorities, some do attain broader and enduring support—so much so that they may become conventional wisdom and cultural orthodoxy. Today no one supports slavery, an issue hotly debated in the nineteenth century. There is now broad consensus on civil rights, universal public education, national responsibility for the health of the economy, environmental protection, social security, and some sort of safety net for the poor. Where a policy consensus is strong, opposition takes the form of controversy at the margins, or a rearguard struggle forced to rely on deception and hypocrisy.[5]

In a free society policy consensus does not speak to "the best way to live," nor does it presume that only one way of life is good. It does not aspire to an "overarching consensus," if by that we mean a single, all-embracing view of what makes people happy or what creates a flourishing community. Policy consensus is pragmatic and problem-centered. Nevertheless, we may discern an underlying coherence, perhaps tentative and incomplete, respecting what makes for a more just society. We should not be too quick to find incoherence, or to presume that differences are necessarily deep, unbridgeable, beyond shared experience and fruitful debate, beyond reconciliation.

Policy consensus is always somewhat messy and impure, in part because it takes account of costs and tradeoffs. To protect fragile coastlines, wetlands, or other ecological treasures, certain kinds of use and enjoyment must be restricted. To encourage conservation of energy, we may offer tax credits for new technologies, thereby limiting public revenues. These tradeoffs are made within and not outside the political process, which is bound to be divisive and may sometimes block collective action. Even when there is agreement about ends, there may be sharp controversy about means. This frustration does not make consensus unattainable, or misty, or unreal. Where consensus exists, and insofar as it exists, it can quiet shrill voices, include more interests, and lead to sounder policies.

Public Goods. Some social benefits crucially depend on collective action and self-restraint. Public safety, health, education, conservation, and many other public goods are at risk when people attend

---

5. This can be seen in partisan debates over Social Security or environmental protection.

only to their own interests, without counting the costs others must bear. Economists call these costs "negative externalities": "externalities" because they lie outside the purview of what rational self-interest seems to require; "negative" in that they create burdens rather than benefits.[6] A factory discharging wastes into a river creates a negative externality by polluting the water used downstream by others; someone who litters a street or schoolyard imposes costs for cleanup and diminishes the quality of public life.

Driven as they are by individual self-interest and short-term considerations, markets cannot be relied on to create or sustain public goods. (See above, chapter 8, p. 94ff.) Such market failures may sometimes be corrected by long-term thinking—as when loggers, looking ahead, plant new trees to replace those they cut, or when competition is suspended for some purposes, such as setting industry-wide safety standards or sharing the costs of research. Some public goods depend on private rather than public decisions. Colleges, museums, orchestras, and hospitals appeal to an interested public for donations, fees, and the support that will justify government subsidies. The cultural resource will be available so long as enough people are willing to pay, or at least participate. Yet public goods suffer (and may be stillborn) when they are hostage to consumer preferences and market-determined costs.[7] Markets work well for the affluent, who can pay for private education or safe and pleasant neighborhoods. But genuine public goods should be available to everyone who needs or wants them.

Art, literature, scholarship, science, education, and religion are especially vulnerable to the coarsening and cheapening effects of mass entertainment and mass marketing. Yet they are vital ingredients of a shared culture, enhancing a community's capacity to produce mature, competent, spiritually whole persons and viable, responsive,

---

6. "Positive" externalities confer benefits, as when a neighborhood is improved as a result of individual efforts, in people's own interests, to maintain clean sidewalks and attractive lawns. It is one of the many ironies of history that self-serving aristocrats and despots left legacies of future museums and open spaces, unwittingly creating positive externalities for the benefit of later generations.

7. For example, in an aging population consumer preferences erode support for public education, and they undermine academic standards when parents and students have other priorities, such as athletics. Market forces affect public goods in other ways as well. Where land is cheap and undeveloped, it is relatively easy to create parks and other public spaces, but it is much harder to do so when costs have escalated.

value-centered institutions. Threats to culture are hard to take seriously if we see only a world of individual satisfactions and unlimited possibilities. Calling attention to those threats may seem hostile (and may sometimes be hostile) to new ideas. This perception reflects much that is good in the modern temper. It is harmful, however, insofar as it disparages the public good of a shared culture.

Culture is not static. We need not bow to conventional ideas about what constitutes art or who belongs in a pantheon of heroes. Instead, we should accept the profoundest mandate of modern thought: that we apply critical intelligence to life's troubles and possibilities. When the quality of culture is in question, the public goods are excellence, creativity, and integrity. These standards are wholly compatible with change and progress, as is shown by the widespread appreciation of modern art. This does not mean that everything is permitted or that all ideas are equally worthy or equally grounded in reason and experience. Without respect for objective standards, and for continuity as well as change, the degradation of culture is inescapable.

Civic Virtue. A long-standing alternative to the liberal ethos is "republican" virtue. Here an ideal of liberty is cherished, but "civic republicanism," as it is sometimes called, gives that ideal a sobering spin. Republican doctrine is based in part on admiration for ancient Athenian democracy and the Roman Republic. Republican ideas were developed during the Renaissance, in connection with the struggle for self-government by the Italian city-states of the fifteenth and sixteenth centuries.[8] Civic republicans believe that freedom is a gift of civic life, to be realized in and through self-government. Liberty is not the pursuit of private interests by detached and self-made individuals. Rather, the core idea is self-government, which calls for action by citizens, in public, together with others, to promote *res publica*, "the public good." A free people is a virtuous people, sustained by institutions that make freedom possible and give it direction.

The republican tradition shares a great deal with liberalism, notably support for the rule of law and constitutional democracy. These ideals envision a free, self-reliant, self-respecting citizenry. In contrast, liberalism divorces freedom from responsibility. In 1775, when

---

8. The republican tradition is examined in J. G. A. Pocock, *The Machiavellian Moment: Florentine Political Thought and the Atlantic Republican Tradition* (Princeton, N.J.: Princeton University Press, 1975). See also Philip Pettit, *Republicanism: A Theory of Freedom and Government* (Oxford: Clarendon Press, 1997).

Patrick Henry cried, "Give me liberty or give me death," he thought of liberty as an expression of civic virtue. "Our brethren are already in the field. Why stand we here idle?" Political liberty, for these Virginians, was freedom to act for the common good. It entailed a willingness to set aside immediate self-interest, if need be to pledge their own "lives, fortunes, and sacred honor." So too, when Thomas Jefferson called "the pursuit of happiness" an "unalienable" right, he was invoking an eighteenth-century doctrine far removed from contemporary claims to unregulated choice and the sovereignty of self.[9]

The cultivation of civic virtue has no secure place in liberal thought. This is because civic virtue calls for something akin to a "civil religion" and the piety it demands. The tenets of a civil religion tell people how they should live interdependent lives. The young must be socialized to accept and internalize appropriate attitudes, understandings, and beliefs. Democracy calls for critical attitudes and sustained debate, but people cannot absorb this ethos without learning the civic virtues of toleration, empathy, and self-restraint. To send the right messages, a culture of civility is required. People in authority—parents, teachers, ministers, and others—do not shrink from saying what are good thoughts and right choices. The cultivation of civic virtue must place some limits on freedom. In the republican tradition this balance is sought with an easy conscience and without apology.

Enlightened Preferences. Democracy and the marketplace are alike in that they honor individual preferences, and do so at some cost to the common good. In a democracy political choices count even if they are ill-informed, unstable, or irrational. Similarly, consumer sovereignty governs in the marketplace: the preferences of consumers are taken as given, studied, and explained by market analysts, but not judged for good sense or moral rightness; what matters is what people want and will buy. Moreover, in ordinary life, most of the time, preferences are respected. This is a feature of civility, which eases the bonds of social life and makes them more supportive. Communitarians share this concern for civility, but they insist that preferences cannot be assessed apart from the contexts within which they are expressed. Some contexts, such as health care, education,

9. Garry Wills, *Inventing America* (New York: Doubleday, 1978), pp. 250–255.

and politics, properly demand close scrutiny of what people prefer and how they justify their preferences.

When we care about outcomes in family life, education, business, or politics, we realize very quickly that what people prefer cannot be a sure guide to high standards and good institutions. Many preferences are self-destructive or show reckless disregard for the safety of others. A well-ordered home, school, or business must balance respect for preferences against the benefits of discipline and the need for cooperation.

The common good requires *enlightened* preferences. We oppose the unregulated pursuit of self-interest and encourage support for public goods, including an informed electorate. We take seriously the difference between what is desired and what is desirable.[10] John Stuart Mill misspoke when he said: "the sole evidence it is possible to produce that anything is desirable, is that people do actually desire it."[11] What people want is indeed very often the best indication of what they need and should have. It is not the "sole" or unimpeachable evidence. We are especially respectful of elementary wants for survival, health, and self-respect. As Mill himself suggests in the passage I have quoted, we must still consider the difference between what is wanted and what is good. Although desires may well be evidence for the desirable, that evidence is never conclusive. What we want is always subject to criticism and amendment in the light of what is good for us or for the worlds we inhabit.

AFFIRMATIVE IDEALS

In a famous essay Isaiah Berlin criticized the view that liberty could be enhanced—made "positive" rather than "negative"—by coercing people to virtue.[12] Berlin insisted on a commonsense understanding of liberty: people are free when they can act voluntarily, without

10. This was a distinction highlighted by Dewey. See John Dewey, *The Quest for Certainty* (1929; reprint, New York: G. P. Putnam's Sons, 1960), p. 260.

11. John Stuart Mill, *Utilitarianism* (1863), in *Utilitarianism, On Liberty, Considerations on Representative Government* (reprint, London: J. M. Dent, 1984), p. 36.

12. Isaiah Berlin, "Two Concepts of Liberty" (1969), in *The Proper Study of Mankind: An Anthology of Essays,* edited by Henry Hardy and Roger Hausheer (New York: Farrar, Straus and Giroux, 1997), pp. 191–242.

coercion or interference. Liberty may be rightfully abridged, as when we are required to wear bicycle helmets, pay taxes, do military service, or be imprisoned upon conviction for a serious crime. These restrictions are justified, but they do not make people more free. Much damage has been done by public intellectuals like Rousseau and Marx, who thought freedom should be redefined to mean something different from (and more noble or morally appealing than) the absence of coercive interference. People are truly free, it is said, when they act in the light of reason, or for the common good or, in Rousseau's enigmatic phrase, in accord with "the general will." Because what these criteria mean is best determined by intellectual, religious, and political leaders, people can be "forced to be free."[13]

This is not a fanciful concern. Many well-intentioned thinkers have disdained the forms of democracy and justice. They have sought "real" democracy and "real" justice, a richer and more profound morality.[14] This contempt for forms may extend to rules regulating the power of government, thereby weakening resistance to despotic regimes. When elementary liberties and due process of law are not prized or are neglected, higher ideals are likely to be at best precarious and even a sham.

This is a good argument, but we should not allow it to undermine commitment to the common good. When we attend only to minimal standards, we shut out more positive, more affirmative, more demanding conceptions of freedom, democracy, and justice. Freedom from interference or coercion is not the best light we can have, not a moral beacon. It does not necessarily give us the will or the capacity to do what is right or to claim what we need. An affirmative conception of freedom is not necessarily the same as (and should not be blackened by) Rousseau's unhappy dictum, or by any other ideological or theological justification for sacrificing basic liberties to an

---

13. "Hence, in order that the social pact shall not be an empty formula, it is tacitly implied in that commitment—which alone can give force to all others—that whoever refuses to obey the general will shall be constrained to do so by the whole body, which means nothing other than that he shall be forced to be free" (Jean-Jacques Rousseau, *The Social Contract* [1762; reprint, London: Penguin Books, 1968], p. 64).

14. Even John Dewey sometimes wrote in this vein, because he wanted to see democracy as a form of communal life and not only as a political system.

allegedly highminded and all-knowing deity, sometimes called "the people." The scary idea that we might be "forced to be free" should have long since lost its power to frighten and mislead. It should not deter us from seeking better ways of being human, better ways of being free. Above all, freedom as an ideal cannot be equated with doing as we please in undisciplined or unregulated ways. Someone obsessed by fantasy, indifferent to responsibilities, easily swayed by the opinions of others, unable to connect means and ends is hardly an autonomous person. Genuine autonomy requires government of the self. We cannot do without the bare bones of liberty, but they need sinews of discipline and social support. Freedom as noninterference—even freedom from domination—is an impoverished ideal, which needs to be enriched by a more complex conception of what liberty is for, what conditions it needs, and how it contributes to the common good.

The Rule of Law. The need for a more positive understanding of political ideals is apparent when we consider the set of principles we call "the rule of law," which I discussed in chapter 9 (see p. 110f). This ideal is often given a narrow and negative meaning, sharply focused on rules limiting the abuse of power by government officials. In the American version, independent judges, acting within a well-established legal tradition, have the last word as to what the law is. However, what a statute or the Constitution requires is always affected by changing attitudes and new learning. The law is meant to be stable, but not static. In the twentieth century, the U.S. Supreme Court, having become more sensitive to changes in moral sentiment, adopted new ways of thinking that led toward a more expansive view of the rule of law, especially in cases affecting due process and legal equality. The Court barred evidence tainted by official misconduct, enlarged the rights of counsel for criminal defendants, and gave new protections to minorities and women. In these and other ways the rule of law was transformed from a set of negative constraints to an affirmative ideal, inseparable from other efforts to define and advance the common good.[15]

15. The upshot is a more "responsive" legal system. On responsive law see Philippe Nonet and Philip Selznick, *Law and Society in Transition: Toward Responsive Law* (1978; reprint, New Brunswick, N.J.: Transaction Publishers, 2001).

RESPONSIBLE PLURALISM

Much experience with the misuse of power has taught us to curb and offset concentrated power. No one can be trusted with unlimited power. The premise of political pluralism is that only power can check power. In keeping with principles they well understood, the framers of the Constitution designed limited and divided government. However, they wanted to make government accountable, not feeble and ineffective. Accordingly, the U.S. Constitution envisions a strong government that also rests, to a large extent, on a healthy civil society. The latter is made up of competing groups, powerful enough to balance one another, strong enough to create a stable framework of enduring institutions. The outstretched arm of government is restrained by the energy and resources of local communities, organized professions, vested interests, and major institutions. Political pluralism was originally a conservative idea, but it was soon absorbed into the liberal tradition. The lesson was clear: freedom is best served when a pattern of countervailing power prevails, when power is dispersed but not fragmented.

The major ideas in pluralist doctrine belong to our common intellectual and moral heritage. This legacy is debased when the common good is taken to be whatever state of affairs emerges from the conflicts and compromises of contending interests. For then the common good is a vector sum of social forces. The latter are thought of as real and palpable, anchored in genuine needs or concerns, the true sources of value and policy. Interest-group pluralism has been conventional wisdom among many contemporary students of the political process. It is, however, offensive to the pluralist foundations of American democracy. The American founders sought a framework within which the public interest would be discovered and pursued. "Factions," as understood by James Madison, would be curbed by inviting the participation of many diverse views and interests, which would check one another.[16] Laws would be passed after due deliber-

---

16. James Madison defined a faction as "a number of citizens, whether amounting to a majority or minority of the whole, who are united and actuated by some common impulse of passion, or of interest, adverse to the rights of other citizens, or to the permanent and aggregate interests of the community" (*The Federalist*, No. 10 [1787; reprint, New York: Bantam Books, 1982], p. 43).

In *The Federalist*, No. 51, Madison argued that "[a]mbition must be made to counteract ambition. . . . This policy of supplying, by opposite and rival interests,

ation, in the light of evidence and argument.[17]

The implicit theory of the U.S. Constitution is best understood as responsible pluralism. The inevitability of faction was recognized, as were its negative effects. By taming faction while welcoming the free play of contending interests, the Constitution would provide for ordered liberty, which would save the nation from populist democracy and unbridled self-interest.

Responsible pluralism restrains partisan conflict by insisting on fidelity to the general welfare. Americans understand the need for partisan controversy, but they reject self-serving maneuvers, bickering, and gridlock. They expect politicians to cooperate and compromise as well as compete. They expect the struggle for power to cease when the country's vital interests are at stake. The ethos of pluralism is not well served by partisan zeal, especially if it includes the politics of deception and of personal destruction.

COLLECTIVE INTELLIGENCE

The common good is not an abstract expression of hope and imagination, not unanchored in social needs, or beyond correction. Nor is it a product of deductive reasoning. The common good should be understood as an unending quest, a collective response to the problems set by new circumstances and new ideas.

Reasoning together is subject to many mistakes, temptations, and corruptions. Not least important is the temptation to treat the common good as an empty slogan, used to advance special interests or to conceal unpopular policies. For this purpose, it helps to keep the common good as vague as possible. We should respond by demanding

the defect of better motives, might be traced through the whole system of human affairs, private as well as public. We see it particularly displayed in all the subordinate distributions of power, where the constant aim is to divide and arrange the several offices in such a manner as that each may be a check on the other—that the private interest of every individual may be a sentinel over the public rights" ([1787; reprint, New York: Bantam Books, 1982], p. 262).

17. See Joseph M. Bessette, *The Mild Voice of Reason: Deliberative Democracy and American National Government* (Chicago: University of Chicago Press, 1994). Bessette's work challenges the view that the legislative process is based on factional, interest-driven negotiation rather than dialogue about policy premises and the common good.

openness, sincerity, and concreteness, insisting on a closer look at glittering generalities, which leave all that matters unsaid.

We can improve collective intelligence by following Dewey's lead in recognizing the interplay of means and ends, and his cautions against false and harmful dualisms. We can also do much to make government more knowledgeable, and therefore more effective.

Means and Ends. During the 1960s and early 1970s many Americans were confused and upset by a sharp dislocation of means and ends. They agreed with the government that the spread of communism should be resisted. As a means to that end, however, the war in Vietnam became increasingly difficult to accept. The military goals seemed less than clear. Were we fighting communism? Intervening in a civil war? Interfering with Vietnam's struggle to be free of foreign domination, first French and then American? Most important, the kind of war being waged was increasingly seen as out of proportion to the nation's objectives. Slowly, troubled by doubt, Americans were made aware of a fundamental principle of morality and statesmanship: We cannot choose goals without determining how they are to be achieved and what costs they entail. When we do not ask these questions, we invite conduct that is likely to be irrational or immoral or both. We may count as costs the casualties of only one side, or fail to recognize as among the costs of doing business such negative externalities as undrinkable water or unsafe products.

The greatest cost is the loss of moral integrity—that is, the capacity to know and the readiness to do what should be done in the light of moral standards. A dangerous symptom is the transformation of what should be a means, chosen with regard to all its effects, into what amounts to an end in itself, taken as a given and immune from criticism. An example is passionate, uncritical loyalty to a religious or political movement. In this and many other instances, the means swallow the end.[18]

Pernicious Dualisms. A pervasive theme in John Dewey's thought is a steadfast objection to the unfruitful dualisms that so often mislead thought and practice. In many of his writings Dewey warned against drawing hard-and-fast lines between mind and body, theory and practice, fact and value. These and other "pernicious dualisms" are ob-

---

18. On the continuum of means and ends, see John Dewey, *Theory of Valuation* (Chicago: University of Chicago Press, 1939), pp. 40–50. For a reprise see *The Moral Commonwealth* (Berkeley: University of California Press, 1992), pp. 328–330.

stacles to thought and good judgment. They get in the way of a community's efforts to deal with its problems in constructive ways.

An example is the supposed opposition of freedom and discipline. To confuse freedom with the rules and commands that set limits and prescribe conduct would be a travesty, worthy of George Orwell's biting irony. But to see freedom and discipline as necessarily opposed is to ignore the many ways in which liberty depends on education, law, and effective organization. In a free society parents try to raise children who will be able to make independent, responsible, self-preserving choices. To do so, however, the parents must give their children direction and support, encouraging some things and discouraging others. The same interdependence of freedom and discipline appears in many spheres of life. The important question is this: what kinds of discipline are needed for what kinds of freedom?

Another dualism is the supposed opposition between public and private life. Although the two realms are properly kept apart for many purposes, they also overlap and intersect. It is a public decision to recognize the special need for privacy in family life, as we do in protecting defendants in a criminal prosecution from a spouse's potentially damaging testimony. Still, rights of privacy are sometimes limited, as when the private lives of "public figures" are exposed in the press.

Many great issues can be dealt with intelligently only by bridging the public-private divide. Thus private property is not necessarily wholly private, untouched and unregulated by public concerns. Private property may be subject to nuisance and zoning ordinances, the public interest in building a highway, or a policy protecting minorities from exclusion.

This preference for permeable boundaries does not mean we should give up self-government in churches, universities, professions, and business enterprises. Each sphere of life has a logic and necessities of its own. However, the separation of spheres cannot be absolute. We cannot build walls of separation from abstract categories. Making clear distinctions is important, but that makes possible—it does not forbid—a fact-based understanding of interactions and connections.

Intelligent Government. In a democracy no claim to expertise is immune from criticism or unchecked by countervailing power. This was another lesson of the Vietnam War, which ultimately sapped public confidence in the foreign-policy and military establishments. After some years of quiescence and trust, during which they gave policy experts the benefit of the doubt, Americans came to their own conclusions about the costs of the war and the good sense of its aims. In the process some hard truths about experts were learned. Insulated policy worlds can make experts prisoners of unquestioned assumptions; claims to special knowledge encourage arrogance and complacency.

For a vital democracy government should be a *competent* instrument of collective will, organized for the pursuit of the common good. This is the responsive government I have mentioned before. A responsive government learns to know the needs, troubles, and aspirations of the people, as well as the changing circumstances that set limits and enlarge opportunities. In the United States much has been done to make government more knowledgeable and therefore more competent. Many agencies, state and federal, collect, analyze, and publish great quantities of information. We do not have, however, a clear conception of the role of social knowledge in responsive government. Distrust creates fear of planning, which frustrates collective intelligence. Knowledge is important for checking power, including power based on expertise. We can speak truth to power when we know how decisions are made, including to whom officials listen and in what ways. Effective scrutiny calls for public participation in government decisions. In this way, knowledge is shared, scrutinized, and enlarged.

A knowledgeable government can do a great deal without intrusive or centralized control, without giving up the benefits of local initiative. In the United States, a good example is the potential role of the national government in public education. The work of the Department of Education should be mainly supportive, without mandating standardized ways of teaching and learning. The federal government can help best by serving as the chief resource for excellence in teaching and administration, including model schools, model texts, well-produced documentaries, science projects, software, and much else that requires exceptional talent and expensive facilities. This strategy would provide the tools needed under modern conditions for successful learning as well as effective local administration. The authority of the materials would derive from their utility and excellence, and not from rules and mandates. This strategy would honor the federal principle and the principle of subsidiarity, reflecting the truth, discussed in chapter 4, that community, properly understood, is a "unity of unities."

CLIO'S TRUMPET

In the pantheon of ancient Greece, among the daughters of Zeus, we meet Clio, muse of history. She is easily recognized by the trumpet she uses to acknowledge the past and herald the future. Tradition has her mainly concerned with fame, victory, and high honor. Perhaps so, but surely the goddess has more important things to say. Her trumpet proclaims the great lessons of history. She is no closet scholar, preoccupied with mute details. Clio dwells among us as an informing presence, shedding light on the past, sketching the future, admonishing us to learn from our mistakes.

Clio's gift to humankind is an appreciation of the common good. She does not say we can draw inexorable conclusions from fixed assumptions about what people need or want, what they will agree to, or what justice requires. Instead, the common good is known in an untidy way, the only way we learn from experience. Our conclusions are necessarily tailored to circumstances, and they are always open to further inquiry and clarifying debate. Clio's truth is won by self-correction, not by the deployment of knockdown arguments.

The Sovereignty of Reason. The communitarian persuasion does not invite a flight from reason into a comforting realm of moral certainty and fidelity to tradition. No retreat is sounded from the quest for a critical morality, which is our best effort to examine, in a scientific spirit, the recurrent troubles and redeeming opportunities of social life. Our steady aim should be to improve and apply collective intelligence. The outcome of our inquiry may confirm, repudiate, or amend a conventional or received morality.

This appeal to reason is wholly compatible with recognition of the worth of beliefs we accept unconsciously and uncritically, and of the special obligations we have to our families or particular communities. A science of morality points just as clearly to the benefits of piety, humility, and loyalty as it does to more abstract or "cosmopolitan" virtues, such as fidelity to science, justice, or the moral equality of all human beings.

Reason is not rationalism, nor should it be equated with rationality understood as abstract thought, long chains of argument, or simplified models of how people behave or think. Reason is empirical as well as theoretical, inductive as well as deductive. A critical morality faithful to experience will readily recognize the tacit knowledge in custom and social practice. Reason calls for an array of intellectual virtues, not only rigor in thought and argument, but prudence, openness, and dialogue as well. Reason is prudent in questioning the pursuit of short-term or narrowly defined goals, in criticizing preferences and governing choices, and in bringing to bear knowledge of multiple values, available opportunities, and unintended effects. Thus conceived, as Clio's child, reason creates a moral framework for thought and action.[19] This is a tradition we can honor, and make our own.

19. In *The Moral Commonwealth* (pp. 57–62) I discussed five pillars of reason: order, principle, experience, prudence, and dialogue. These ideas are informed by a distinction between reason and rationalism.

CHAPTER 11

A COMMON FAITH

With some license for interpretation, and a few friendly amendments, I have sought to provide, in the preceding chapters, a faithful rendering of the communitarian perspective. In this concluding chapter, however, I may be reaching beyond the communitarian consensus. I expect some dissent from my argument that there is a close connection between religious teachings and communitarian ideas. Nevertheless, the topic cannot be ignored. Too much that is fundamental is shared. As John Dewey made clear in his own essay *A Common Faith,*[1] it would be strange indeed if we could learn nothing from religious experience. What we learn will surely enrich our self-understanding; it will also caution us against religious follies and aggression.

Communitarian principles do not stand alone. They draw credence and support from fundamental understandings of human nature and the human condition. When we ask why we honor the principle of moral equality, or why should we care about future generations and about other people's well-being, we enter realms of faith and understanding, where philosophy and theology meet and interact. Together they make clear, and should also govern, our self-defining choices. Those choices are often mistaken, corrupt, and self-defeating.

---

1. John Dewey, *A Common Faith* (New Haven: Yale University Press, 1934).

Made wisely, however, they create a legacy of well-founded precepts, which are sometimes made explicit by a Buddha or an Aristotle, by Jesus, Calvin, Hobbes, or Kant. Or they may be only dimly perceived, crudely expressed, or followed but not acknowledged.

We honor such precepts when we put away immature thoughts and longings; when we accept the inevitability of death; when we appreciate the difference between narrow and broad self-interest; when we strive to negotiate, in good faith, the competing obligations of kinship and citizenship. This legacy helps us understand what attitudes and beliefs, what articles of faith, what lessons of history underpin a communitarian morality. Our answer must take us into the minefields of religious doctrine, and find a way out as well.

AFFIRMING THE PRINCIPLE OF COMMUNITY

In 1861, as the Civil War was about to begin; in 1863, at Gettysburg; and in 1865, as the war drew to a close, Abraham Lincoln sought to define and sustain the American political community. He found a unifying symbolism in religious belief: "Both [sides] read the same Bible and pray to the same God. Each invokes His aid against the other." At a time of bitter enmity and unremitting slaughter, Lincoln's speeches conveyed a message of reconciliation, framed by a determination to save the Union and do "the right as God gives us to see the right." At his first inauguration, in 1861, he said, "We are not enemies, but friends. We must not be enemies." These sentiments appealed to the conscience of a people who would seek, "under God," "a new birth of freedom." President Lincoln brought religion to the fore, and he did so even as southern churches defended slavery and prayed for the success of the Confederacy.

This rhetoric was wholly appropriate. Every known society has looked to religion for comfort, coherence, and moral redemption. Religion helps people make sense of a world beyond their control, enriches cultures and causes communities to flourish, creates strong identities and passionate loyalties. Much evil has been justified in God's name: superstition, bigotry, priestly oppression, genocide. Nevertheless, religious sentiments cannot be dismissed as vestiges of a prescientific age, sustained by primordial awe, fear of the unknown, and yearning for immortality. Religions retain their appeal, and their warrant, because they foster self-scrutiny, self-transcendence, loyalty, and humility. These are the virtues and strengths of piety, which, as filial love, sustains the obligations of family life. Other forms of piety are patriotism, religious observance, institutional loyalty, friendship, discipleship, and vocational pride. Each draws people to the sources of their being—that is, to the attachments from which they derive a sustaining identity. Piety is a prima facie or presumptive good, beneficial in many contexts but not necessarily good in all forms or circumstances. Some forms of piety ask too much of us, and for the wrong objects, or claim immunity from criticism, or demand undivided and unconditional loyalty. Therefore, piety is tempered by the more dispassionate virtues of civility. Piety demands conformity and justifies exclusion, while civility welcomes diversity, encourages toleration, and legitimates controversy. Civility builds frameworks within which people can cooperate despite their divergent views and interests.[2]

Here is another importance difference between the liberal ethos and the communitarian persuasion. Liberalism has made much of civility but has had a hard time appreciating the benefits of piety. For communitarians, piety and civility complement one another.[3] Together they produce sensitive, self-preserving communities.

In Buddhism, Hinduism, Christianity, Judaism, and Islam, individualism is rejected, even abhorred.[4] All the religions enjoin compassion and caring; all call for awareness of interdependence. Yet the gifts of forgiveness, enlightenment, and salvation are offered to individual persons. In each person a spark of divinity is found, which is a way of saying each person has intrinsic worth. In these beliefs we can readily discern that union of solidarity and respect I referred to earlier as the principle of community.[5]

2. For more on civility and piety, see *The Moral Commonwealth* (Berkeley: University of California Press, 1992), chap. 14. There (p. 391) I argue that civility and piety, though different, are interdependent. Civility is based on respect, not love, but *deep* respect blurs the line between civility and piety.

3. The First Amendment upholds civility by prohibiting an "establishment of religion," and piety by barring laws that inhibit "the free exercise" thereof.

4. Although Protestant Christianity is often associated with individualism, notably in Max Weber's *Protestant Ethic and the Spirit of Capitalism*, and in R. H. Tawney's *Religion and the Rise of Capitalism*, this argument applies to the unintended effects of Protestant doctrine, not to the religious ideas themselves, or to the experience of belonging to a Protestant sect or congregation.

5. See chapter 2, p. 26f. It may be said of the Protestant Reformation that it was an effort to readjust the balance between solidarity and respect.

In Christian thought the principle of community is well expressed in the idea of neighborly love. Echoing passages in the Hebrew Bible,[6] Jesus taught: "Love thy neighbor as thyself." What kind of love is neighborly love? Who is my neighbor? An answer is found in the parable of the Good Samaritan. My neighbor is a particular person who rightfully claims my fellow feeling, my mercy, charity, and support. By neighborly love we do not mean love for "humanity" or "mankind," for people in general or in the abstract. The object of moral concern is an individual human being, especially one whose life has touched our own in important ways. This is the source of special obligation, which is not limited to kin or fellow townsmen or colleagues. In the parable a special connection was created by the accident of proximity, of being present at the scene of distress.[7] The lesson is that people are to be valued as unique persons, entitled as such to respect and care. Insofar as we lose touch with that particularity, the principle of community is weakened or rejected.

In this demanding doctrine, every human being is potentially a neighbor, and every neighbor claims our active concern. This moral imperative exquisitely—and achingly—combines "universalist" and "particularist" ideals. The combination is fragile, the tension is irrepressible. Religions are pulled in both directions. They speak for humankind, but do so in a local idiom, cabined by culture and corrupted by pride.

Can we have piety without religion? Can we appreciate the nuances of human interaction, the constraints and opportunities of the human condition, without theological reflection and learning? In theory, yes. But we should be wary of distancing ourselves from ideas and traditions that have sensitively explored and often improved the quality of collective life.

FAITH, GOD, AND MORAL TRUTH

The world of religion and theology is full of enigmas, which befog the claims of faith and the meaning of "God." People can share the

---

6. See Leviticus 19:18.

7. Paul Ramsay, *Basic Christian Ethics* (Chicago: University of Chicago Press, 1950), pp. 94–95. See also Jeremy Waldron, "On the Road: Good Samaritans and Compelling Duties," *Santa Clara Law Review* 40 (2000): 1053–1103.

same religion despite wide differences in how they experience ritual, profess belief, or accept dogma. Today we must still attend to the venerable distinction between the "esoteric" theological arguments of sophisticates and the "exoteric" faith of more naive believers. It is not easy to know just what people mean when they say they believe in God or in the teachings of a sacred text. Belief takes many forms and is often accompanied by unspoken reservations. A biblical narrative may be interpreted as an allegory rather than accepted as straight history. Every key religious idea—including concepts of the soul, salvation, resurrection, or the afterlife—can be given symbolic rather than literal meanings. Each may be understood without relying on supernatural entities, events, or explanations. The moral and spiritual truths expressed may be understood as psychological as well as theological; their authority may rest on experience rather than divine command or revelation. In some religious communities, such as Roman Catholicism, the authority to teach and interpret is vested in a priestly hierarchy.[8] Elsewhere more leeway is allowed for diversity and autonomy in belief and worship. Everywhere belief is entwined with legend, metaphor, and myth.

It is perhaps shocking but true that people can be religious without believing in God. Being religious has more to do with practice than belief: affiliation, observance, ritual, attitudes of reverence and respect. Furthermore, religious practice is largely determined by unchosen identities, formed mainly in childhood. Religious piety builds upon the pieties of kinship, ancestry, and ethnicity.

According to Martin Buber, the Jewish philosopher and theologian, God is a "masterpiece of man's construction."[9] This thought is faithful to the spirit of modernism, which glorifies *homo faber*, "man the maker." But it would be wrong to suppose that whatever is a "human construction" is necessarily superficial, readily altered, incapable of being a compelling framework for thought and action. This would be a misreading of ordinary life, and of the great arenas of human achievement as well. Science is a human construction, so is high art, so is constitutional government. We do not disparage

8. In the Roman Catholic Church, this authority is tempered, to some extent, by institutional and ideological divisions within the Church, so that it is easy to discern liberal and conservative schools, orders, and publications.

9. Martin Buber, *Eclipse of God: Studies in the Relation between Religion and Philosophy* (New York: Harper Torchbooks, 1952), p. 62.

divinity when we say it is a human creation. In its best forms this "construction" invests an animal species with ennobling virtues, transcendent ideals, and moral responsibility. To glimpse God or speak with God is to reach for a realm beyond conditioned, contingent, fallible humanity to one perceived as eternal and unconditioned. God stands for moral perfection and disinterested love, for unblemished harmony and unlimited power. All these absolute powers and perfections are denied to humans, who are notoriously weak, short-lived, and self-seeking. Yet the perfections are by no means alien to the human condition. They are criteria for judging our frailties, trespasses, and distractions. This capacity for judgment and yearning for judgment may be what we mean by the oft-noted spark of divinity in humankind.

It is a common mistake to suppose that an idea or practice is "merely" symbolic. Anything that conveys meaning is symbolic, but some symbols have much greater human significance than others. Many are useful conveyors of meaning only if they have very specific referents or denotations; like a computer language, such symbols may be readily changed or discarded. Similarly, we do not care very much about traffic signals, so long as they work. Symbols have a richer meaning when they are expressive of personality or culture; when they convey subtle, often open-ended or connotative meanings; when they fix identities and thereby make possible a potent union of self and culture. Expressive symbolism does much to determine the springs of action and the quality of life. It is not "merely" anything.

Allegories and parables, rhetoric and poetry, holy days and ceremonies: these and many other forms of ardent symbolism transform moral abstractions into articles of faith. They bind belief to symbolic experience. Every society finds ways of bridging the gap between knowing something abstractly and making that knowledge a sure guide to conduct. A moral code calls for commitment and resolve as well as understanding. Articles of faith may rest on knowledge, and may be tested and changed in the light of experience. But to be fully realized in the choices people make, those articles must be sustained and enriched by beliefs that cut deep and form selves.

Although God can be described in many ways (perhaps as beyond human knowledge or comprehension), the most helpful way, it seems to me, associates God with moral truth. Indeed, it could be said that, at least in one major manifestation, God is moral truth made incarnate and expressed as revelation. Here incarnation refers to an idea embodied in living traditions, rituals, teachings, and institutions.[10]

What are these truths deemed worthy of allegiance as articles of faith? Here are a few thoughts on that subject, chosen to show the affinity of religious beliefs and the communitarian persuasion.

Most important is the principle of moral equality, which I have discussed earlier in connection with social justice (chapter 9, p. 111f) and as the foundation of communitarian respect for individuals as persons (chapter 4, p. 41f). Moral equality finds religious expression in the idea that humans are "children of God" or "made in the image of God." Each is in some sense equally valuable, equally worthy of concern and respect. This principle can be justified without relying on theology, by pointing to the evils that ensue when moral equality is diminished or rejected, such as hostile discrimination and caste privilege. But those evils are recognized as such not only because of the sufferings they impose, but also because they violate our deepest convictions about the respect human beings deserve. A corollary is that we recognize no moral elites. Every human being, however powerful, saintly, or well educated, is corruptible; everyone is capable of self-scrutiny, self-restraint, self-respect, and love.[11]

A more sobering moral truth is the pervasive presence of self-interest, pride, and idolatry in human affairs. These are signs of human frailty and finiteness compared to the unlimited life, power, and perfection of God. This doctrine can be restated as a naturalist theory of human nature and of the human situation, more or less as presented by Freud. But the expression of these truths in sacred texts and symbols brings a deeper realization and, very often, a more subtle understanding of sin and redemption.

In this book I have stressed, in various ways, the communitarian awareness of self-interest and overreaching. I have pointed out that even when self-interest is narrowly understood, as selfish and short-sighted, it can be and is an indispensable spur to cooperation and commitment. In analyzing democracy, we do not reject self-interest

---

10. In the *Oxford English Dictionary* one meaning of *incarnate* is "to put into, express, or exhibit in a concrete or definite form; to realize, actualize, embody (an idea or other abstraction)."

11. We know there are exceptions, as in the case of young children or psychopathic personalities, but we disregard the exceptions in embracing moral equality as an article of faith.

as a reason for voting one way rather than another. Yet we do not shrink from asking how the will of the people is to be governed. We do not fail to consider what rules may be necessary to protect the integrity of voting or of political speech. The religious premise, shared by the framers of the U.S. Constitution, is that only in God can there be a union of power and perfection. In human institutions no such union is contemplated or admitted. We come to this conclusion as a result of much experience. The lesson is better understood and more greatly prized when it is part of a broader vision. That vision does not separate the study of God from the study of humanity.

A genuinely realistic understanding of humankind looks beyond our shortsightedness and depravity. These are serious failings, against which we seek defenses; they are the main concerns of "moral realism."[12] But a realistic philosophy recognizes potentials as well as limits. What people can achieve, or aspire to, is just as surely part of human nature, just as surely summoned by the human condition, as are more negative traits and dispositions. The big difference is that we cannot *rely* on the human inclination to recoil from evil and "choose life." We cannot count on disinterested love, even in its natural home, among close relatives. Yet the potential for such love remains an indispensable resource for human betterment.

Here we must depart, to some extent, from the main teachings of Reinhold Niebuhr, one of the twentieth century's great Christian theologians. The polemical context of his writings—the main target of his criticisms—was what he thought of as the excessive optimism of religious thought and moral philosophy. He thought his liberal-minded contemporaries underestimated the pervasiveness of self-interest, pride, rationalization, and the temptations of power. Instead, he argued, our institutions and policies must take account of these failings, recognizing the need for socially mandated coercion and especially the political truth that, in the end, only power can check power. According to Niebuhr, we cannot deal with evil unless we treat it as an ever present threat, in many different guises; unless we see it clearly and guard against it.

Niebuhr opposed the liberal ideas, then prevalent among religious

---

12. Among contemporary writers "realism" can have two different meanings. Moral realism can refer to a doctrine about moral truth, holding that it is in some sense objective, or it can refer to the more commonsense understanding of being "realistic" about ideals and conduct.

as well as secular thinkers, that education and good will, by themselves, can bring social harmony and moral progress. Niebuhr argued forcefully against utopian illusions, which offered new ways of justifying evils in the name of the good.[13]

Despite these warnings, Niebuhr never gave up a dream of social justice. He was a staunch supporter of the New Deal and other liberal programs. In practice, he accepted the need for a constructive, self-preserving combination of realism and idealism. He ended his *Moral Man and Immoral Society* with the predictable comment that man cannot achieve "perfect justice." However, Niebuhr added the thought that social justice is "a very valuable illusion" because "justice cannot be approximated if the hope of its perfect realization does not generate a sublime madness in the soul. Nothing but such madness will do battle with malignant power and 'spiritual weakness in high places.'"[14]

Moral realism offers only a partial view of the human condition. By itself it cannot be a sound guide to personal life or to the design of institutions. This is because moral realism yields only a baseline morality, preoccupied with guarding against evils and disciplining unruly passions. A preoccupation with realism cannot sustain a flourishing existence, which calls for a life guided by hopes as well as fears, by confidence as well as skepticism.

Realism tempered by idealism encourages attitudes of criticism and demands for reconstruction, especially self-criticism and self-reconstruction. We look to the promise of our institutions, not only their limiting premises; to opportunities as well as perils.[15] Discerning the opportunities offered by history, and responding to them, is a worthy spur to moral and political development.

The most demanding expression of moral idealism is the biblical injunction, "Love one another." To say that the law of human life is love seems wildly unrealistic. However, we should think of this

13. For example, illusions fostered by Marxism and "socialism" in the Soviet Union, or hopes of a world without coercion.

14. Reinhold Niebuhr, *Moral Man and Immoral Society* (1932; reprint, New York: Scribner, 1960), p. 277. I am indebted to Lewis Mudge for calling my attention to this passage.

15. In interpreting the U.S. Constitution, for example, we should welcome the idea that the broad concepts and clauses ("the freedom of speech," "due process of law," "equal protection of the laws") contain promises to be made good for future generations of Americans, in the light of new circumstances and understandings.

article of faith as a practical guide to personal life and social policy. We cannot expect wholly disinterested love or other forms of moral perfection, but we can embrace policies that reflect a strong preference for reconciliation, forgiveness, and the overcoming of sentiments of exclusion, revenge, and domination. The law of love can be applied in every sphere of life, in families, business, government, education, religion—wherever, indeed, divisive forces routinely emerge and stubbornly recur. The law of love is a master ideal guiding us to standards and strategies appropriate to particular settings, such as teaching, lawyering, or business practice.

Neighborly love draws us toward individual persons who have unique histories and circumstances. This primacy of the particular becomes apparent when we consider what it means to do justice. The most visible face of justice is the principle of treating people as equals. Like cases are treated alike. An ethic of impersonal judgment prevails. But love and justice are by no means alien realms. Indeed, love is another face of justice, which appears when doing justice must take account of particular circumstances and practical outcomes. The closer we come to finding the right category—a certain kind of offender in a certain state of mind—the closer we come to judging people as persons, in their particularity. Tough love is not precluded. Some form of discipline may be precisely what a particular child or offender may require. But because tough love tempts us to self-righteousness and abuse of power, it should be administered with caution and with adequate safeguards.

The moral truth we call the law of love speaks to all the ways lives are made whole by genuine communication, caring, and respect for differences. The outcome is not perfection. Rather, it is a basis for negotiating the distance between a pristine article of faith and the recalcitrant realities of social life.

The Religious Dimension. Moral truths may be justified by secular principles, such as general welfare or utility, or by the idea that obligation should stem from consent, or by the claim that certain rights are "unalienable." It is easy to show that these and other liberal tenets have religious *origins*. Writing in the seventeenth century, John Locke invoked God freely as the true author of moral truth. Notions of human dignity, equality, and frailty became part of Western culture in and through religious teachings. Secular versions of moral truth came from the schools and closets of Greek and Roman philosophers.

Just because an idea has religious origins does not make it religious. Indeed, moral truths are warranted, not necessarily by religion, but by our best understanding of human experience, including mortality, interdependence, and conflict. This understanding is what matters. One may argue that Christian ethics is preferable to another moral theory, such as the utilitarianism of Jeremy Bentham, or that of Mill or Kant. In such an argument, the choice is between one moral philosophy and another, or perhaps some hybrid. A defense of Christian ethics does not counterpose the divinity of Yahweh or Jesus to the more earthbound claims of Bentham, Mill, Kant, or Dewey. Instead we ask which philosophy (if any) gives the best account of moral experience.

What is it, then, that makes a moral theory religious? The answer must be found in how moral principles are perceived and adopted. Especially important is sustained self-scrutiny, informed by the belief that there is or can be a connection between limited, frail humanity and another realm, somehow beyond time and space, worthy of reverence, awe, and worship. A moral truth becomes an article of faith when it takes on this spiritual significance.

The benefits of religion are offset and undone when it fosters bigoted fear and supine obedience. Nevertheless, it would be self-defeating to give up the benefits of a religious sensibility, reflected in myth, poetry, and narrative as well as systematic theology. Whatever we may think of prophets, messiahs, priests, and shamans, we cannot forget or forgo the Hebrew quest for moral redemption, Isaiah's cry for justice, the law of love expounded by Jesus, the moral courage and prophetic zeal of Mahatma Gandhi and Martin Luther King Jr. For them, moral truths, such as the meaning and limits of civil disobedience, belong to a broader conception of how God and human beings converse.

John Dewey spoke to this larger vision when he distanced himself from "militant atheism," which he though exhibited a want of that "natural piety" he saw in reverent respect for human interdependence, and for the continuities of man and nature.[16] For Dewey, a religious attitude treats ideals as latent in experience, hence wholly "natural." We can and should strive for "a working union of the ideal and the actual." This religious attitude invests the world with

16. Dewey, *A Common Faith*, p. 53.

meaning. It calls for solidarity, not estrangement, for loyalty and love, not alienation.[17]

SPIRITUAL WELL-BEING

In the great religious traditions, believers seek a state of grace—that is, a sense of harmony and fulfillment based on devout adherence to Torah, or to the teachings of Buddha, Confucius, Krishna, Muhammad, or Jesus. Signs of grace are humility and good will or, as some say, purity of heart. More than correct belief is wanted, more also than righteous conduct. Spiritual well-being is evidenced by self-knowledge, commitment, discipline; by wisdom to discern ideal possibilities in nature, including human nature. The wished-for state is a righteous *person*. Righteous *acts* are not enough.

A precondition is psychic competence, especially the capacity to defer gratification, accept responsibility, and care for others. These building-blocks of ordinary life underpin but do not realize the promise of moral well-being. Beyond is a more challenging realm, within which we discover better ways of being human.

The linchpin is self-transcendence. Although this ideal has been expressed in many different ways, the underlying message is much the same. Among Jews, Christians, and Muslims, self-transcendence is a readiness to "let God's will be done." The sovereignty of human will is decisively rejected. No individual, no democratic majority, no statesman, no judge has the last word.[18] A higher law can always be invoked. Buddhism questions the very idea of selfhood; desire is the taproot of evil; boundaries between self and others, self and nature, self and cosmos are blurred if not erased. Yet moral responsibility is upheld. Individuals have to accept and perhaps make amends

17. In a review of Dewey's *A Common Faith*, Reinhold Niebuhr said that Dewey's "credo" "was closer to the primary tenets of prophetic religion than Dewey would be willing to admit." His "is the kind of faith which prophetic religion has been trying to express mythically and symbolically by belief in a God who is both creator and judge of the world. . . . It is questionable whether the kind of supernature . . . against which Dewey protests is really the kind of supernature about which really profound prophetic religion speaks" (*The Nation*, September 25, 1934).

18. Although judicial independence is an important element of the rule of law, it should be noted that judges are not independent of—indeed, they are properly creatures of—legal institutions and a legal tradition.

for their unchosen identities, and they are accountable for the self-defining choices they make in the course of their lives.[19]

Self-transcendence is not necessarily religious. Attitudes of reverence and readiness for self-sacrifice serve many secular purposes and ideals, including the demanding standards of craftsmanship, professional ethics, institutional loyalty, and community service. Religious or not, the importance of these attitudes shows that the morality of self-transcendence is hardly an absence of self-regard, still less an extinction of self.[20] Rather, a work of self-construction goes on, investing the self with appropriate ways of thinking and feeling. In its best forms, spiritual counseling connects caring for oneself and caring for others. This is a bridge hard to build without articles of faith. The latter may not be explicitly religious, but the kinship is close and should be acknowledged.

A main cause of spiritual misery is the condition we call alienation: estrangement from self, work, humanity, or God. Prophets of all sorts have warned that alienation from God is the most serious of human pathologies. Lives are damaged by lost moorings, by drift and moral distraction. Alienated people are vulnerable to self-abasement and to self-destruction. This theme was given a secular, sociological interpretation by Emile Durkheim in his study of *anomie,* a social condition in which lives are ungoverned by supportive rules. For Karl Marx, alienation from work and self was capitalism's most grievous sin.

These ideas remind us that spiritual well-being must be a prime concern of social policy. Its secular significance is recognized by our commitment to liberal education, including support for the arts. Why do we care about enhancing opportunities for education that goes beyond basic skills and job-related training? The great aim of liberal education is to give students the tools they need to live lives enriched by knowledge of history, literature, science, and other cultures. For us it is an article of faith that liberal education will bring special satisfactions and abilities. Students should participate in realms

19. "Making amends" speaks, for example, to the obligations of people who are born rich. I also have in mind the obligations of present-day Americans and Germans for the historical travesties of chattel slavery and the Holocaust. They are not "guilty," but they are properly ashamed and share liability for apologies and reparations.

20. See my discussion of "Buddhist Self-regard" in *The Moral Commonwealth,* pp. 223–227.

of value that would otherwise be closed to them; a spirit of critical affirmation should prevail. What is worthy of appreciation, such as a scientific attitude or the premises of democracy, will be explored and respected. What deserves criticism will be pointed out. The criticism is responsible if it is based on knowledge of alternative possibilities and of the limits and tradeoffs people have accepted or tried to overcome.

This secular quest for spiritual well-being is frustrated when militant fundamentalism claims special knowledge and special authority. Therefore, liberal education must distance itself from religion in some important ways. Nevertheless, religion cannot be banished from liberal education, as something alien and subversive. We are open to religious ideas and intuitions when we are aware of the subtle ways human life is examined in religious myth, allegory, and sacred teachings.

If we care about the spiritual well-being of individuals, we must also care about their moral and cultural environments. A striking feature of human culture is what Gertrude Jaeger and I once called a "strain toward the aesthetic."[21] Cultural symbols are intensified, and made more effective, when they are expressed in music, literature, painting, sculpture, and architecture. Aesthetic experience is an integral part of social life, and that life is diminished when art is set apart or debased.[22] Here is the most revealing connection between spiritual well-being and the quality of culture. The artist's work is necessarily a personal expression of insight, emotion, and skill. But aesthetic experience has a broader reach. It enriches participation in social life by lifting people out of the self-constricting routines and drab practicalities of everyday life. For this reason, at least, art and faith have been closely associated.

PRIVATE AND PUBLIC RELIGION

The American founders were by no means hostile to religion. They took for granted that religion had a vital part to play in a moral com-

---

21. Gertrude Jaeger and Philip Selznick, "A Normative Theory of Culture," *American Sociological Review* 29 (October 1964): 663.
22. This is John Dewey's argument in *Art as Experience* (1934; reprint, New York: Capricorn Books, 1958).

munity. They found ways of giving public support to at least some religious activities. For example, as it moved to open the western territories, the first Congress said, in the Northwest Ordinance, that "religion, morality, and knowledge" are "necessary to the good government and happiness of mankind."[23]

This friendly attitude was limited, however, in two important ways. The framers of the Constitution denied to the new federal government authority to establish a state-sponsored church. The states were free to do so if they wished, but the national government could not tax people to support a particular religion. In the nation as a whole, religious plurality was expected and accepted. A corollary was the view that everyone should be free to believe and worship according to "conscience," without let or hindrance by government. These principles faithfully reflected the ethos of Protestantism, which was prevalent in the newly independent colonies.

This association of religion with conscience has had the unintended effect of "privatizing" religion. If religion is a matter of conscience, then it should be free from public control and walled off from public policy. If, as has been suggested, the sacredness of life is a religious question, then people should be free to make up their own minds about contraception and abortion.[24] Except for protection of that freedom, the issue should be outside the realm of public debate, beyond the jurisdiction of public officials.

This privatizing strategy makes sense for some vital aspects of religion, such as ritual, holy days, and theological arguments regarding, say, the unity or plurality of God. The approach is not helpful, however, where religious and secular beliefs overlap, notably the view that the life of every human being has intrinsic worth and should be protected by law. In applying this principle, we may need consensus on what constitutes a human being and whether a woman's fertilized ovum is actually or only potentially such a human being. We cannot evade the question by relegating it to a private realm and private choice.

Religious ideas, energies, and institutions make major contributions to public morality. Most important is the work of defining

---

23. For further details see A. James Reichley, *Religion in American Public Life* (Washington, D.C.: Brookings Institution, 1985), p. 93.

24. See Ronald Dworkin, *Life's Dominion: An Argument about Abortion, Euthnasia, and Inidvidual Freedom* (New York: Knopf, 1993), chap. 2.

and reinforcing fundamental values: human dignity and responsibility, humility and self-restraint, obligations to family and community, caring for future generations and for the vulnerable and the disadvantaged, ideals of stewardship and reconciliation. The religious traditions do not accept moral indifference, nor is autonomy a basic value. No individual, no institution can claim exemption from God's commands; salvation is not won by invoking the lesser gods of business, politics, art, or science.

Yet religions are often called upon to mind their own business, leaving public morality to law and politics; priests, ministers, and rabbis are to attend to the spiritual lives of their congregations. Indeed, religions lose their innocence and step out of bounds when they ignore the difference between upholding a value and determining public policy. A religious commitment to family, equality, or forgiveness may run up against other concerns, such as public safety. Religion contributes to public morality mainly by holding up a mirror to social life and, in a prophetic spirit, recalling people to their fundamental commitments.

A prison ministry does not try to tear down the walls. It can, however, look beyond the spiritual needs of individuals by scrutinizing sentencing guidelines and prison administration, with a view to resisting draconian penalties and inhumane custody. Such a ministry will accept the realities of discipline and the limits of rehabilitation, but it should be ready to challenge official views of what alternatives are possible and what goals can be achieved. In this way, and in similar ways, religion becomes the conscience of the community.

When religious institutions try to help people in need, they rightly suspect that the needs are spiritual as well as material. This conviction often guides the social service and educational work of so-called "faith communities." These activities are prized by communitarians, not only for the immediate good they do, but also because they strengthen civil society. At the same time, the communitarian principle of inclusiveness is put at risk. Religious institutions are likely to emphasize the spiritual power of their own beliefs, their own rituals. Moreover, they want to protect their own identities in various ways, perhaps by staffing their agencies with co-religionists. Clients may be called on to betray their own religious identities in exchange for much needed help. The larger community may reasonably accommodate a religious group's need for a coherent identity, by allowing preferences in hiring staff and by recognizing the authority of a religious hierarchy or governing board. For its part, the faith community should be inclusive, serving without discrimination, without regard for religious affiliation, without demanding religious participation, above all, without messages of bigotry and hate. These are not hard pills to swallow, at least among those who accept the principle that strangers as well as kinsmen are owed compassion and love.

THE ECUMENICAL MOMENT

The common faith we seek embraces the spirit of *E pluribus unum*, "one out of many." We say yes to plurality even as we uncover convergent truths. A rich variety of beliefs and forms of worship should be accepted and supported, as it largely is in the United States. At the same time the unifying themes within diverse religions and secular philosophies should be known and respected. These demands make sense of modern history, which has created an "ecumenical moment." In other words, ecumenism is an idea whose time has come, prepared for by the heavy costs of religious strife and by the well-understood benefits of mutual respect and constructive dialogue.

Human differences are appreciated most keenly, and welcomed most sincerely, when they testify to an underlying unity. Our common humanity generates diverse ways of life, including different ways of imagining divinity. That same humanity produces cultural universals, such as the centrality of kinship, art and music, the prevalence of wickedness and compassion, reverence and self-transcendence, and much else that human societies have in common.[25] That humans are One as well as Many is a faith that leads to "moral hospitality," a hallmark of the ecumenical spirit.[26]

An ecumenical program is often understood as interchurch rather than interreligious. The main concern is to break down barriers to

25. On cultural universals see A. L. Kroeber and Clyde Kluckhohn, *Culture: A Critical Review of Concepts and Definitions* (New York: Vintage Books, 1963), pp. 349–350.

26. On moral hospitality see Lewis S. Mudge, *The Church as Moral Community: Ecclesiology and Ethics in Ecumenical Debate* (New York: Continuum, 1998), pp. 107–108.

Christian unity: among Roman Catholics, Anglicans, Episcopalians, and Greek Orthodox communities; among Presbyterian, Methodist, and other Protestant affiliates of the World Council of Churches. This limited ecumenism raises few questions about the foundations of faith.

More broadly understood, ecumenism is interreligious. The discussions look beyond specific beliefs, rituals, or ecclesiastical authority. No organic or institutional unity is contemplated. Instead, the quest is for a deeper understanding of the animating principles of Hindu, Buddhist, Jewish, Muslim, or Christian traditions. We approach the varying beliefs and rites with open hearts and inquiring minds. The diverse traditions are taken as given and not meant to be overcome. Everyone involved is self-consciously religious, comfortable with divinity, accustomed to liturgy, familiar with pastoral responsibilities.

A sterner test faces the ecumenical ideal when more secular views are in play, such as those we associate with "secular humanism." This is a naturalist faith, informed by the view that moral truths are grounded in and tested by the funded experience of human communities. It is secular in that it opposes received religions insofar as they cling to literal beliefs about supernatural beings. This secular vision loses clarity, however, when conceptions of God become more abstract and philosophical, more concerned with "first principles" than with the precepts and exploits of Yahweh, Vishnu, or Buddha. In much of theology, since at least the late Middle Ages, the gulf between religious and secular argument has narrowed. When thought moves from God to the *idea* of God, the boundary between philosophy and theology is indistinct.

Although a militant naturalism will surely reject religion, a more authentic and generous version is open to all of human experience, which includes many varieties of deification and worship. Naturalism does not reduce mind to matter, love to attachment, law to power, religion to fantasy. These modalities interact in important ways, and the connections may be strong or weak, benign or harmful. The variable connections between, say, love and sex, or justice and power do not entitle us to deny the reality or ignore the human significance of love or justice or religious experience. Thus, naturalism is not necessarily at odds with religion, and it need not treat religion as an illusion or just a mistake.

Humanist naturalism is especially open to religious ideas. As

Dewey understood it, humanist naturalism is more than a defense of scientific attitudes. His humanity-centered naturalism discerns ways of assessing the quality of human life. An example is the criterion of growth, which Dewey associated with enlarged horizons and improved competences, notably the capacity to live in cooperation with others while gaining and using critical intelligence. In the pragmatist tradition this is an article of faith.

When different religions and philosophies engage in constructive dialogue, they must do so with civility. There can be no privileged truth, no privileged claims to moral authority. When public issues are discussed, a special theological or symbolic idiom must be set aside or bracketed in favor of a common language and shared understandings. To find common ground, people must be able to understand one another. This does not mean they cannot or should not draw on their own ways of thinking when coming to conclusions or talking among themselves. An internal or parochial conversation may bring enrichment as well as solidarity, and at some point its subtleties may be ripe for entry into public discourse. But dialogue is meant to build bridges, not walls.

Earlier I mentioned the complementary values of civility and piety. A few more words may be helpful here. Civility is a richer, more demanding idea than "being civil," which may require no more than taking turns and allowing other voices to be heard *without a serious effort to really listen.* Genuine civility strives to make sense of an unfamiliar idiom and will be disinclined to give it an unattractive interpretation. An ecumenical program honors piety as well as civility. Norms of civility presume differences and demand respect. Piety builds on shared origins, histories, and fates. Working together, civility and piety strengthen dialogue and shared understanding.[27]

27. The two come together when we adopt what Robert Post has called "civility rules," which enjoin respect for persons, practices, and institutions while expressing a shared understanding of what is at stake for the community and for the integrity of its components. In *Constitutional Domains* (Cambridge, Mass.: Harvard University Press, 1995), Post explores the significance of "civility rules" for various legal issues, including privacy and free speech. Civility rules uphold civility by governing how people treat one another, thereby protecting the integrity of individual persons, who belong to a community yet are separate as well. At the same time, these rules are expressions of piety in that they confirm shared meanings and understandings, and shared histories.

The interplay of civility and piety is a recurrent subtext in this book, a theme that captures much that I have said about community and communitarian thought. Civility draws us outward, to embrace strangers, appreciate differences, and regulate conflict. Piety looks inward toward shared identity and consciousness of kind. The two imperatives often compete, as when we insist on values that revise traditions and transcend locality. The larger truth, however, is that civility is naked without articles of faith, which tell us who we are and what we live by, and piety without civility is debased and out of control.

INDEX